D1482214

888 Hints for the Home

888 ASTUCES pour AMÉNAGER son INTÉRIEUR

888 Tipps für Ihr Zuhause

888 Woonideeën

888 ideas para diseñar el hogar

888 idee per la casa

888 dicas para o lar

888 Tips för hemmet

888 Hints for the Home

888 ASTUCES pour AMÉNAGER son INTÉRIEUR

888 Tipps für Ihr Zuhause

888 Woonideeën

888 ideas para diseñar el hogar

888 idee per la casa

888 dicas para o lar

888 Tips för hemmet

KÖNEMANN
is an imprint of
Frechmann Kolón GmbH
www.frechmann.com

© 2014 for this edition: Frechmann Kolón GmbH

Editorial project: LOFT Publications
Barcelona, Spain
Tel.: +34 932 688 088
Fax: +34 932 687 073
loft@loftpublications.com
www.loftpublications.com

Editor:
Daniela Santos Quartino

Editorial coordinator:
Simone K. Schleifer

Assistant to editorial coordination:
Aitana Lleonart Triquell

Art director:
Mireia Casanovas Soley

Design and layout coordination:
Claudia Martínez Alonso

Layout:
Anabel N. Quintana

Cover layout:
María Eugenia Castell Carballo

Translations:
Cillero & de Motta, Mengès (FR)

ISBN 978-3-86407-428-8 (GB)
ISBN 978-2-8099-1074-2 (Mengès, France)
ISBN 978-3-86407-426-4 (D)
ISBN 978-3-86407-429-5 (NL)
ISBN 978-3-86407-427-1 (E)
ISBN 978-3-86407-430-1 (PORT)
ISBN 978-3-86407-479-0 (SWE)

Printed in Spain

Few things are as stressful and as exciting as moving house. Empty spaces create the same anxiety that an artist suffers in front of a blank canvas. So much to do and so many possibilities!

So, beyond the style that the house will have – which is very important to establish from the outset –, there are a number of guidelines that can help us to optimally distribute the spaces, to efficiently position the fittings and successfully organize the furniture.

All these ideas are reflected in this book, which covers, chapter by chapter, the different living spaces, and includes tips, tricks and advice on decorative details and the colors and textures suitable for any area of the house.

Peu d'expériences sont aussi stressantes et excitantes à la fois que celle qui consiste à changer de maison. Les espaces vides provoquent la même anxiété que celle qu'éprouve un artiste devant la toile blanche. Tout est à faire et il y a tellement de possibilités !

C'est la raison pour laquelle, au-delà du style qu'il est important de choisir dès le début, il existe une série de modèles pouvant nous aider à optimiser la distribution des espaces, à placer les équipements aux meilleurs endroits et à organiser l'emplacement du mobilier.

Cet ouvrage parcourt, chapitre par chapitre, les différentes pièces, offrant suggestions, astuces et conseils sur la décoration, les couleurs et les matériaux adaptés.

Wenige Dinge sind so anstrengend und gleichzeitig aufregend wie ein Umzug. Leere Räume lösen dieselbe innere Unruhe aus, die ein Künstler vor einer weißen Leinwand empfindet. Es ist so viel zu tun, und es gibt so viele Möglichkeiten!
Deshalb gibt es neben dem Stil, in dem die Wohnung gestaltet werden soll, - und es ist wichtig, darüber von Anfang an zu entscheiden - eine Reihe von Richtlinien, die uns dabei helfen können, die Räume optimal aufzuteilen, die Einrichtung effektiv zu gestalten und die Möbel so aufzustellen, dass wir uns wohlfühlen.
Alle diese Ideen sind in diesem Buch vereint, das Kapitel für Kapitel die verschiedenen Räume der Wohnung durchgeht, und sie werden mit Ideen, Tricks und Ratschlägen zu dekorativen Details, geeigneten Farben und Texturen für jede Fläche des Hauses ergänzt.

Weinig dingen zijn zo stressvol en opwindend tegelijkertijd als verhuizen. Lege ruimtes roepen dezelfde angst op als die een schilder voelt voor een wit doek. Alles moet nog gemaakt worden en er zijn zo veel mogelijkheden!
Daarom zijn er, naast de stijl die de woning zal hebben - en waarover al in het beginstadium moet worden beslist - een aantal richtsnoeren die ons kunnen helpen om de ruimtes optimaal in te delen, de voorzieningen op efficiënte wijze te plaatsen en de woning naar tevredenheid in te richten.
Al deze ideeën zijn opgenomen in dit boek, dat per hoofdstuk de verschillende vertrekken van de woning bij langs gaat en ideeën, trucs en tips geeft over decoratieve details en de geschikte kleuren en texturen voor iedere willekeurige ruimte van de woning.

Pocas cosas resultan tan estresantes y excitantes a la vez como cambiarse de casa. Los espacios vacíos generan la misma ansiedad que sufre un artista frente al lienzo en blanco. Todo por hacer y ¡tantas posibilidades!...

Por eso, más allá del estilo que tendrá la vivienda -y que es importante decidir desde el principio-, hay una serie de pautas que pueden ayudarnos a distribuir óptimamente los espacios, a situar eficientemente el equipamiento y a organizar satisfactoriamente el mobiliario.

Todas estas ideas se recogen en este libro, que recorre, capítulo a capítulo, los diferentes espacios de la vivienda, y se complementa con ideas, trucos y consejos sobre detalles decorativos y los colores y texturas idóneos para cualquier superficie de la casa.

Poche cose causano contemporaneamente tanto entusiasmo e stress come cambiare casa. Gli spazi vuoti creano la stessa ansia di un artista davanti alla tela bianca. C'è tutto da fare e le possibilità sono infinite!

Per questo, al di là dello stile che avrà l'abitazione – che è importante definire sin dall'inizio – vi sono una serie di punti da seguire che possono aiutarci a distribuire in modo ottimale gli spazi, a posizionare in modo efficace i vari elementi e a organizzare al meglio gli arredi.

Tutte queste idee sono raccolte in questo libro che, capitolo per capitolo, analizza i vari spazi della casa ed è arricchito da idee, trucchi e consigli su dettagli decorativi, colori e materiali adatti a qualsiasi superficie.

Poucas coisas são, em simultâneo, tão stressantes e excitantes como mudar de casa. Os espaços vazios geram a mesma ansiedade que um artista sofre frente à tela em branco. Tudo por fazer e tantas possibilidades!

Por isso, para além do estilo que a habitação terá – e que é importante decidir desde o princípio –, existe uma série de regras que podem ajudar-nos a distribuir optimamente os espaços, a situar eficientemente o equipamento e a organizar satisfatoriamente o mobiliário.

Todas estas ideias estão reunidas neste livro, que percorre, capítulo a capítulo, os diferentes espaços da habitação, e é complementado com ideias, truques e conselhos sobre detalhes decorativos e sobre as cores e texturas idóneas para qualquer superfície da casa.

Få ting er så stressende og spændende på en gang som indretning af hjemmet. De tomme rum skaber den samme følelse som en kunstner foran en blankt lærred. Man kan gøre lige hvad man vil, og har tusind muligheder.

Udover at man bør vælge stil fra begyndelsen findes der en række retningslinier som kan hjælpe med at udnytte pladsen optimalt, og placere møbler og udstyr tilfredsstillende og effektivt.

Alle de ideer er samlet i denne bog, som omhandler de forskellige rum i hjemmet afsnit for afsnit sammen med tips, ideer og gode råd om farver, teksturer og dekorative detaljer til hele huset.

LIVING ROOM
SALON
WOHNZIMMER
ZITKAMER
SALÓN
SALOTTO
SALA
VARDAGSRUMMET

To define the living room in spaces shared with other areas of the house, organize the space around these three basic elements: a sofa, coffee table and rug.

Pour délimiter le salon dans un espace partagé avec d'autres zones de la maison, il faut maintenir les proportions entre les formes de ces trois éléments de base : le canapé, la table basse et le tapis.

Um das Wohnzimmer von anderen Bereichen innerhalb der Wohnung abzugrenzen, sollte man die Proportionen zwischen diesen drei Grundelementen beachten: Das Sofa, den Couchtisch und den Teppich.

Om de zitkamer binnen ruimtes die gedeeld worden met andere entourages van de woning af te bakenen, moeten de juiste proporties van de vormen van deze drie basiselementen te worden aangehouden: de bank, de zitkamertafel en het vloerkleed.

Para definir el salón en espacios compartidos con otros ambientes de la casa conviene mantener las proporciones entre las formas de estos tres elementos básicos: el sofá, la mesa de centro y la alfombra.

Per definire il salotto in spazi condivisi con altri ambienti della casa, si consiglia di mantenere le proporzioni tra le forme di questi tre elementi di base: divano, tavolino centrale e tappeto.

Para definir a sala em espaços partilhados com outros ambientes da casa convém manter as proporções entre as formas destes três elementos básicos: o sofá, a mesa de centro e o tapete.

För att definiera vardagsrummet i utrymmen som delas med andra funktioner i hemmet är det viktigt att behålla proportionerna mellan formerna på dessa tre grundläggande beståndsdelar: soffan, soffbordet och mattan.

Fit a mirror behind the couch that fills the entire wall to dramatically create the feeling of spaciousness in the living room. This tip is only suitable for minimalist ambiences, as otherwise the space would be too overelaborate.

Placer un grand miroir sur tout le mur derrière le canapé permet d'augmenter de façon spectaculaire la sensation d'espace dans le salon. Cette astuce n'est valable que dans les pièces minimalistes, sinon elle pourrait provoquer un effet final trop chargé.

Bringen Sie hinter dem Sessel einen Spiegel an, der die gesamte Wand einnimmt. Dadurch wirkt das Wohnzimmer sehr viel größer. Dieser Trick ist nur für Zimmer geeignet, die minimalistisch eingerichtet sind, im anderen Fall wirkt der Raum überfüllt.

Plaats een spiegel die de hele wand achter de fauteuil inneemt, zodat het lijkt alsof de zitkamer veel groter is. Deze truc is alleen geschikt voor minimalistische vertrekken omdat de ruimte anders te vol lijkt.

Coloca un espejo que ocupe toda la pared detrás del sillón para que se multiplique de forma espectacular la sensación de espacio en el salón. Este truco es solo apto para ambientes minimalistas, ya que de lo contrario el ambiente resultaría muy recargado.

Sistema uno specchio che occupi tutta la parete dietro la poltrona in modo da moltiplicare in modo spettacolare la sensazione di spazio nel salotto. Questo trucco è adatto solo agli ambienti minimalisti; negli altri tipi di arredi l'ambiente risulterebbe eccessivamente carico.

Coloque um espelho que ocupe toda a parede atrás do sofá para que a sensação de espaço na sala se multiplique de forma espectacular. Este truque só é aplicável em ambientes minimalistas, visto que de contrário o ambiente ficaria muito sobrecarregado.

Placera en spegel som täcker hela väggen bakom fåtöljen. På så sätt blir känslan av rymd mycket större i vardagsrummet. Detta råd passar bara i minimalistiska miljöer. Vid det motsatta kan intrycket bli att rummet är mycket belamrat.

Take advantage of irregularities in the house to install certain furniture or equipment, such as the stove and space to store wood.

Les dénivelés de la maison peuvent accueillir certains meubles ou équipements comme le poêle et servir d'espace de rangement pour le bois.

Nutzen Sie Niveauunterschiede in der Wohnung aus, um bestimmte Möbel oder Gegenstände wie den Ofen und Feuerholz unterzubringen.

Maak van de niveauverschillen in het huis gebruik om bepaalde meubels of gebruiksvoorwerpen, zoals de kachel, neer te zetten of om brandhout op te slaan.

Aprovecha los desniveles de la casa para instalar determinados muebles o equipamiento, como la estufa y el espacio para almacenar la leña.

Sfrutta i dislivelli della casa per inserire mobili o altri elementi, come la stufa e lo spazio per conservare la legna.

Aproveite os desníveis da casa para instalar determinados móveis ou equipamento, como o recuperador de calor e o espaço para arrumar a lenha.

Använd husets nivåskillnader för att placera vissa möbler eller föremål där, som en kamin eller förvara veden där.

Take advantage of an opening in the walls of the living room to fit shelves (glass if possible to allow light to pass freely between the rooms).

Une ouverture dans les murs du salon peut accueillir des étagères en verre permettant à la lumière de circuler librement.

Nutzen Sie eine Öffnung in der Wohnzimmerwand, um Regale aufzustellen. Diese sollten aus Glas sein, damit sie Licht in die Räume lassen.

Benut openingen in de wanden van de zitkamer om planken te bevestigen. Maak deze van glas voor meer lichtinval tussen de verschillende ruimtes

Aprovecha una apertura en las paredes del salón para colocar estantes, y procura que éstos sean de cristal para que permitan pasar la luz libremente entre los ambientes.

Sfrutta l'apertura nella parete del salotto per sistemarvi dei ripiani; opta per il vetro che consente il passaggio della luce da un ambiente all'altro.

Aproveite uma abertura nas paredes da sala para colocar prateleiras, e procure que estas sejam de vidro para que permitam passar a luz livremente entre os ambientes.

Använd dig av en öppning i vardagsrummets väggar för att hänga upp hyllor och se till att de är av glas så att ljuset kan flöda mellan de olika utrymmena.

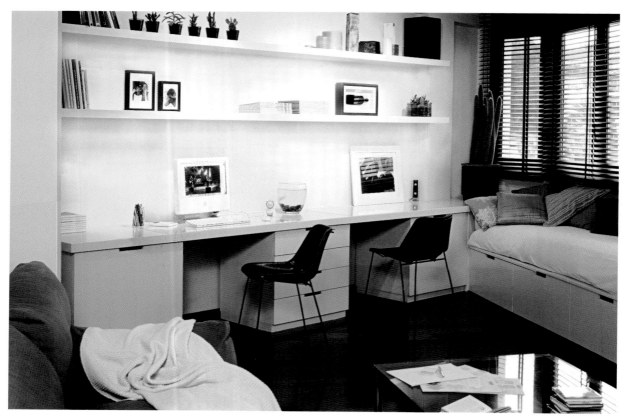

Make the bottom shelf of the bookcase wider so that it can be used as an office desk.

On peut monter une étagère plus large dans la partie basse de la bibliothèque pour la transformer en table de travail.

Bringen Sie unterhalb des Bücherregals ein breiteres Regalbrett an, das Sie als Schreibtisch benutzen können.

Plaats een bredere plank onderaan de boekenkast, die dienst kan doen als tafel voor de werkruimte.

Coloca una balda más ancha en la parte de debajo de la librería para convertirla en una mesa para el espacio de trabajo.

Sistema una mensola più ampia nella parte inferiore della libreria per trasformarla in un tavolo da usare come spazio di lavoro.

Coloque uma prateleira mais larga na parte de baixo da estante para a converter numa mesa para o espaço de trabalho.

Placera en bredare hylla i bokhyllans nederdel så att den kan användas som arbetsplats.

Install a shelf about 15.8 inches off the floor in a corner of the living room that you can use as a table or bench.

Installer une étagère dans un coin du salon à environ 40 cm du sol permet de gagner une surface utilisable comme petite table ou banquette.

Installieren Sie in einer Ecke des Wohnzimmers in ca. 40 cm Höhe ein Regalbrett. Sie gewinnen damit eine Fläche, die Sie als Beistelltisch oder Bank nutzen können.

Installeer een plank op ongeveer 40 cm van de vloer in een hoek van de zitkamer. Zo krijgt u een extra oppervlak dat gebruikt kan worden als tafeltje of bank.

Instala una balda a unos 40 cm del suelo en un rincón del salón y ganarás una superficie que se puede usar como mesita o banco.

Inserisci una mensola a circa 40 cm da terra, in un angolo del salotto, per ottenere una superficie utilizzabile come piccola seduta o panca.

Instale uma prateleira a cerca de 40 cm do chão num canto da sala e ganhará uma superfície que se poderá usar como mesita ou banco.

Placera en hylla ungefär 40 cm från golvet i ett hörn av vardagsrummet, som kan användas som bord eller bänk.

Create more storage space on the wall behind the sofa. Choose a shelf length equal in length or longer than the sofa and install it high enough so that it does not get in the way.

Le mur occupé par le canapé permet d'optimiser l'espace de rangement. On choisit une étagère d'une largeur égale ou supérieure à celle du canapé et on la monte à une hauteur suffisante pour éviter de s'y cogner.

Nutzen Sie die Wand, an der sich das Sofa befindet, um Stellplatz zu gewinnen. Suchen Sie ein Regalbrett aus, das genauso lang oder länger als das Sofa ist, und bringen Sie es hoch genug an, dass man sich nicht daran stoßen kann.

Gebruik de muur waar de bank tegenaan staat als extra opbergruimte. Kies een plank die net zo lang of nog langer is dan de bank en plaats hem hoog genoeg zodat niemand zijn of haar hoofd stoot.

Aprovecha la pared que ocupa el sofá para ganar espacio de almacenamiento. Escoge una balda con un largo igual o superior al del sofá y colócala lo suficientemente alta para evitar golpes.

Sfrutta la parete utilizzata dal divano per guadagnare spazio di contenimento. Scegli una mensola di larghezza pari o superiore al divano e sistemala in posizione sufficientemente alta da evitare di urtarla.

Aproveite a parede que o sofá ocupa para ganhar espaço de arrumação. Escolha uma prateleira com um comprimento igual ou superior ao do sofá e coloque-a suficientemente alto para evitar bater nela.

Använd den vägg där soffan står för att få mer förvaringsutrymme. Välj en hylla som är lika lång eller längre än soffan och placera den högt för att undvika att man slår sig.

Fit open shelves for ornaments and hide objects and toys that would make the space look messy behind doors.

Vous pouvez disposer les objets de décoration sur des étagères ouvertes et ranger à l'intérieur les papiers, les jouets et d'autres éléments qui donneraient un aspect désordonné à l'espace.

Lassen Sie einige Fächer der Schrankwand für Ziergegenstände offen, und bewahren Sie hinter den Türen Papiere, Spielzeug und Gegenstände auf, die dem Zimmer sonst ein unordentliches Aussehen geben würden.

Zet accessoires op de planken en bewaar papieren, voorwerpen en speelgoed die het vertrek een slordig uiterlijk geven achter de deuren van het meubelstuk.

Deja los estantes abiertos para los adornos y guarda tras las puertas del mueble papeles, objetos y juguetes que darían un aspecto desordenado al espacio.

Lascia i ripiani aperti per i soprammobili e riponi dietro le ante del mobile carta, oggetti e giochi che trasmetterebbero un senso di disordine.

Deixe as estantes abertas para os adornos e guarde atrás das portas do móvel papéis, objectos e jogos que dariam um aspecto desordenado ao espaço.

Lämna de öppna hyllplanen åt dina prydnadssaker och förvara papper, föremål och leksaker bakom dörrarna på möbeln, för att inte ge ett oordnat intryck.

Sofas with integrated shelves are perfect to have useful objects such as throws, remote controls and books near at hand.

Les canapés avec tablettes intégrées sont très utiles pour garder sous la main les objets les plus utilisés au salon comme les couvertures, les télécommandes et les livres.

Sofas mit eingebauten Fächern sind sehr praktisch, um häufig gebrauchte Gegenstände, wie Decken, Fernbedienungen und Bücher zur Hand zu haben.

Banken met geïntegreerde planken zijn een grote bondgenoot om de meest gebruikte voorwerpen in de zitkamer, zoals dekens, afstandsbediening of boeken, bij de hand te hebben.

Los sofás con estantes integrados son un gran aliado para tener a mano los objetos de mayor uso en el salón, como mantas, mandos y libros.

I divani con ripiani integrati sono un grande alleato che consente di avere sempre a portata di mano gli oggetti di maggiore utilizzo in salotto, come coperte, telecomando e libri.

Os sofás com estantes integradas são um grande aliado para ter à mão os objectos mais utilizados na sala, como mantas, comandos e livros.

Soffor med inbyggda hyllor är till stor hjälp om man vill ha filtar, fjärrkontroller och böcker nära till hands.

Create a living room that is both modern and elegant: let the sofa or the armchairs add color to the room and keep the rest of the space within the same range of contrasting tones.

Comment créer un salon élégant et moderne : la touche de couleur apportée par le canapé ou les fauteuils contraste avec les autres éléments de la pièce qui appartiennent à une même gamme de couleurs.

Gestalten Sie ein elegantes und zugleich modernes Wohnzimmer: Verleihen Sie ihm durch das Sofa und die Sessel eine farbige Note, und halten Sie den übrigen Raum in einem einheitlichen, kontrastierenden Ton.

Creëer een elegante en tegelijkertijd moderne zitkamer: laat de bank of de stoelen voor een kleurig accent zorgen en houd de rest van de ruimte binnen hetzelfde contrasterende kleurengamma.

Crea un salón elegante y moderno a la vez: deja que el toque de color lo aporten el sofá o los sillones y mantén el resto de la estancia en una misma gama de tonos que contrasten.

Crea un salotto elegante e moderno allo stesso tempo: lascia che ad apportare colore siano il divano e le poltrone; mantieni il resto degli elementi in una stessa gamma di toni in contrasto.

Crie uma sala simultaneamente elegante e moderna: deixe que o toque de cor fique a cargo do sofá ou das poltronas e mantenha o resto da divisão com uma mesma gama de tons que contrastem.

Skapa ett elegant och modernt vardagsrum: låt soffan eller fåtöljerna stå för färginslaget och låt resten av rummet vara i en kontrasterande färgskala.

To enhance a living room in which one tone is dominant, choose a sofa with a contrasting color.

Pour rehausser la couleur d'un salon où domine une seule tonalité, on choisit un canapé ayant une couleur qui contraste avec celle-ci.

Um den einheitlichen Ton des Wohnzimmers hervorzuheben, wählen Sie für das Sofa eine kontrastierende Farbe.

Kies voor een bank in een contrasterende kleur om een zitkamer waarin een kleur overheerst beter te doen uitkomen.

Para realzar un salón en el que domina una sola tonalidad, elige un sofá con un color que contraste.

Per vivacizzare un salotto in cui domina una sola tonalità, scegli un divano con un colore contrastante.

Para dar realce a uma sala na qual predomina uma só tonalidade, escolha um sofá com uma cor que contraste.

För att förhöja intrycket av ett vardagsrum där en nyans dominerar, kan man välja en soffa i en kontrastfärg.

Go for prints on the sofa but keep to the same range of colors for the rest of the furniture and fittings

Vous pouvez oser les imprimés pour votre canapé mais vous devez respecter la même gamme de couleurs pour les meubles et les équipements restants.

Haben Sie Mut zu einem Sofa mit gemustertem Bezug, aber halten Sie die anderen Möbel und Einrichtungsgegenstände im gleichen Farbton.

Durf met bedrukte stoffering in de bank, maar houd daarbij hetzelfde kleurengamma aan als de rest van de meubels en gebruiksvoorwerpen.

Atrévete con los estampados en el sofá pero mantén la misma gama de colores en el resto de los muebles y en el equipamiento.

Osa con le stampe sul divano, ma mantieni la stessa gamma di colori nel resto degli elementi e degli arredi.

Atreva-se com os estampados no sofá, mas mantenha a mesma gama de cores nos restantes móveis e no equipamento.

Våga välja en mönstrad soffa, men använd samma färgskala i resten av möblerna och inredningen.

Use fabrics as a decorative element. Simply changing the combination of cushions, throws and rugs is enough to give a living room a makeover.

Les tissus deviennent des éléments de décoration. Le salon peut changer d'aspect facilement en coordonnant différemment les coussins, les couvertures et les tapis.

Nutzen Sie Textilien als dekorative Elemente. Es genügt einfach die Kissen, Decken und Teppiche auszuwechseln, um dem Wohnzimmer ein neues Aussehen zu verleihen.

Neem uw toevlucht tot stoffering als decoratief element. Door simpelweg de combinatie van kussens, dekens en vloerkleden te veranderen, geeft u de zitkamer een nieuw uiterlijk.

Recurre a los textiles como elemento decorativo. Cambiando simplemente la combinación de cojines, mantas y alfombras es suficiente para dar una nueva apariencia al salón.

Ricorri ai tessuti come elemento decorativo. Cambiando semplicemente la combinazione di cuscini, coperte e tappeti potrai dare un nuovo aspetto al salotto.

Recorra aos têxteis como elemento decorativo. Alterar simplesmente a combinação de almofadas, mantas e tapetes é o suficiente para dar uma nova aparência à sala.

Använd dig av textilier som dekorativt inslag. Genom att byta ut kombinationen av kuddar, filtar och mattor kan man enkelt ge vardagsrummet ett nytt utseende.

A side table is both functional and decorative. Therefore, when choosing it we can unleash our creativity and recycle pieces that acquire a new use.

La table d'appoint a aussi bien une fonction pratique que décorative. Par conséquent, vous pouvez donner libre cours à votre créativité en recyclant des éléments auxquels vous attribuez un nouvel usage.

Der Beistelltisch ist sowohl nützlich als auch dekorativ. Deshalb können wir bei dessen Auswahl unserer Kreativität freien Lauf lassen und Gegenstände recyceln, die nun eine neue Verwendung finden.

Een bijzettafel is zowel functioneel als decoratief. Laat daarom bij de keuze uw creativiteit de vrije loop en recycle onderdelen die op een andere manier kunnen worden aangewend.

La mesa auxiliar es tan funcional como decorativa. Por eso, al elegirla podemos desatar nuestra creatividad y reciclar piezas, que adquieren un nuevo uso.

Il tavolino aggiuntivo ha sia un ruolo funzionale che decorativo. A tal fine, scegliendola potremo dare sfogo alla nostra creatività e riciclare dei pezzi che acquistano così un nuovo uso.

A mesa auxiliar é tão funcional como decorativa. Por isso, ao escolhê-la podemos soltar a nossa criatividade e reciclar peças que assumem uma nova utilização.

Avlastningsbordet är såväl dekorativt som funktionellt. Släpp loss din kreativitet och återanvänd föremål på ett nytt sätt.

Transparent side tables have the major advantage of not affecting the style of the room. The most important thing is not to place them in areas where they will get in the way.

Les tables d'appoint transparentes ont le grand avantage de ne pas interférer avec le style du salon. Le plus important est de ne pas les placer dans les zones de passage pour qu'elles ne gênent pas la circulation.

Durchsichtige Beistelltische haben den großen Vorteil, dass sie den Stil des Wohnzimmers nicht beeinträchtigen. Das Wichtigste ist, sie nicht so aufzustellen, dass sie den Durchgang nicht behindern.

Doorzichtige bijzettafels hebben als grote voordeel dat ze de stijl van de zitkamer niet beïnvloeden. Het belangrijkste is om ze niet in loopruimtes te plaatsen, zodat ze de doorgang niet belemmeren.

Las mesas auxiliares transparentes tienen la gran ventaja de no afectar el estilo del salón. Lo más importante es no colocarlas en zonas de paso para que no lo entorpezcan.

I tavolini aggiuntivi trasparenti hanno il grande vantaggio di non influenzare in alcun modo lo stile del salotto. La cosa importante è evitare di sistemarli in zone di passaggio in modo da non creare intralcio.

As mesas auxiliares transparentes têm a grande vantagem de não afectar o estilo da sala. O mais importante é não as colocar em zonas de passagem para que não se tornem um obstáculo.

Genomskinliga sidobord har den stora fördelen att de inte påverkar vardagsrummets stil. Det viktigaste är att inte placera dem i genomgångsområden så att de inte är i vägen.

Make the most of the living room area by converting it into a multifunctional space. Place shelves that do not exceed the height of the backrest behind the sofa.

On peut rentabiliser les mètres carrés du salon en le transformant en un espace multifonctionnel, avec des étagères derrière le canapé qui ne dépassent pas la hauteur du dossier.

Nutzen Sie die Fläche des Wohnzimmers und verwandeln Sie es in einen Vielzweckraum. Bringen Sie Regale hinter dem Sofa an, die nicht höher als die Rücklehne sind.

Benut de vierkante meters van de zitkamer door ze in een multifunctionele ruimte om te vormen. Zet boekenkasten achter de bank die niet hoger zijn dan de rugleuning.

Rentabiliza los metros cuadrados del salón convirtiéndolo en un espacio multifuncional. Coloca estanterías detrás del sofá sin que superen la altura del respaldo.

Sfrutta al massimo i metri quadrati del salotto trasformandolo in uno spazio multifunzione. Sistema dei ripiani dietro il divano, evitando che superino l'altezza dello schienale.

Rentabilize os metros quadrados da sala convertendo-a num espaço multifuncional. Coloque estantes atrás do sofá sem que superem a altura do encosto.

Utnyttja hela vardagsrummets yta genom att förvandla det till ett rum med många olika användningsområden. Placera bokhyllor bakom soffan som inte är högre än dess ryggstöd.

A coffee table with wheels can be easily moved and placed where it is required or where it does not get in the way.

Une table basse à roulettes peut être déplacée facilement et mise à l'endroit le plus utile ou, dans ce cas, le moins gênant.

Ein Couchtisch mit Rädern kann leicht dahin verschoben werden, wo man ihn am meisten braucht oder wo er am wenigsten stört.

Een salontafel op wieltjes is gemakkelijk te verplaatsen, zodat u hem daar kunt neerzetten waar u hem nodig heeft, of juist waar hij het minst in de weg staat.

Una mesa de centro con ruedas se puede desplazar con facilidad y colocar donde más interese, o en su caso, donde menos moleste.

Un tavolino centrale dotato di ruote può essere facilmente spostato e riposizionato dove si desidera, o se necessario, dove dia meno fastidio.

Uma mesa de centro com rodas pode deslocar-se com facilidade e ser colocada onde for mais conveniente ou, se for o caso, onde menos incomode.

Ett soffbord på hjul kan enkelt förflyttas och placeras var man vill eller där det inte är i vägen.

In ambiences with neutral tones, hang different colored curtains on one window to create an interesting play of light in the room.

Dans un intérieur aux tons neutres, vous pouvez choisir pour une même fenêtre des rideaux de couleurs différentes, créant ainsi un jeu de lumière intéressant dans la pièce.

In Räumen mit neutralen Farbtönen hängen Sie an einem Fenster verschiedenfarbige Vorhänge auf, um ein interessantes Lichtspiel im Zimmer zu schaffen.

Hang in ruimtes met neutrale kleurschakeringen voor hetzelfde raam gordijnen in verschillende kleuren op, voor een interessant lichtspel naar binnen toe.

En ambientes de tonos neutros instala cortinas de diferentes colores sobre una misma ventana para crear un interesante juego de luces hacia el interior de la estancia.

Negli ambienti dai toni neutri aggiungi tende di vari colori a una stessa finestra per creare un interessante gioco di luci verso l'ambiente interno.

Em ambientes de tons neutros instale cortinados de diferentes cores numa mesma janela para criar um interessante jogo de luzes no interior da divisão.

I rum med neutrala färger kan man placera gardiner i olika färger i ett och samma fönster för att skapa ett ljusspel in mot rummet.

Create a balanced environment. Draw an imaginary horizontal line along the walls and do not used colored elements above the top half of the line.

Vous pouvez créer un ensemble équilibré, en évitant de placer des éléments de couleurs au-dessus d'une ligne imaginaire horizontale tracée sur les murs du salon.

Schaffen Sie eine ausgeglichene Atmosphäre. Ziehen Sie eine imaginäre horizontale Linie an den Wänden entlang und bringen Sie keine farbigen Elemente oberhalb dieser Linie an.

Zorg voor een evenwichtige sfeer. Trek een denkbeeldige horizontale lijn langs de muren en laat kleurelementen niet meer dan de helft van de lijn innemen.

Crea un ambiente equilibrado. Traza una linea imaginaria horizontal a lo largo de las paredes y no dejes que los elementos de color ocupen la mitad superior de la línea.

Crea un ambiente equilibrato. Traccia una linea immaginaria orizzontale lungo le pareti e non lasciare che gli elementi colorati occupino la metà superiore della linea.

Crie um ambiente equilibrado. Trace uma linha imaginária horizontal ao longo das paredes e não permita que os elementos de cor ocupem a metade superior da linha.

Skapa en harmonisk miljö. Dra en inbillad horisontell linje längs väggarna och låt inte de färgglada elementen vara ovanför den linjen.

Use curtains to separate spaces or as screens. They can be hung from a thin metal rod attached to the ceiling or on rails.

On peut utiliser les rideaux comme élément de séparation de l'espace ou comme paravent, les accrochant à une fine barre métallique fixée au plafond ou à des tringles.

Benutzen Sie die Vorhänge auch als Trennwände oder Wandschirme. Man kann sie von einer schmalen Metallleiste oder Schienen, die an der Decke befestigt werden, hängen lassen.

Maak ook gebruik van gordijnen of kamerschermen om ruimtes van elkaar te scheiden. Deze kunnen met een dunne metalen stang of rail aan het plafond worden bevestigd.

Utiliza las cortinas también como separadores de ambientes o biombos. Se pueden colgar de una fina barra metálica fijada al techo o en rieles.

Usa le tende anche per separare ambienti o come paraventi. Puoi appenderle a una sottile sbarra metallica fissata al soffitto o a delle guide.

Utilize as cortinas também como separadores de ambientes ou biombos. Podem ser penduradas numa fina barra metálica fixa ao tecto ou em calhas.

Använd också gardiner som rumsavskiljare eller skärmar. Man kan hänga dem från en smal metallstång i taket eller i skenor.

Instead of placing a floor lamp on the side table in the corner, choose a low-hanging light fixture. In this way, the light covers a wider area.

Au lieu de placer une lampe sur pied sur la petite table d'appoint à l'angle de la pièce, vous pouvez accrocher une lampe au plafond et la faire descendre très bas : la lumière rayonnera ainsi sur une surface plus vaste.

Statt einer Lampe auf dem Beistelltisch in der Ecke wählen Sie eine Deckenlampe und hängen Sie sie sehr tief. Auf diese Weise hat das Licht einen größeren Radius.

Kies, in plaats van een staande lamp op het bijzettafeltje in de hoek voor een plafondlamp en laat deze heel laag hangen. Op die manier wordt het licht beter verspreid.

En lugar de situar una lámpara de pie en la mesita auxiliar del rincón, elige una lámpara de techo y colócala a una altura muy baja. De esta manera, la luz abarca un radio más amplio.

Invece di posizionare una lampada con la base sul tavolino aggiuntivo in angolo, opta per un lampadario a soffitto facendolo scendere molto. In tal modo la luce si diffonderà su un raggio maggiore.

Em vez de colocar um candeeiro de pé na mesita auxiliar do canto, opte por um candeeiro de tecto e coloque-o a uma altura muito baixa. Desta forma, a luz abrange um raio mais amplo.

Istället för en bordslampa på vardagsrummets avlastningsbord kan man välja en taklampa och hänga den lågt. På så sätt sprids ljuset inom en större radie.

Place a floor lamp beside the sofa: it is great for reading and also creates an intimate, warm atmosphere.

Mettre un lampadaire à côté du canapé facilite la lecture et crée une atmosphère intime et accueillante.

Stellen Sie eine Stehlampe neben dem Sofa auf: Sie ist sehr praktisch zum lesen und erzeugt außerdem eine intime, gemütliche Atmosphäre.

Zet een staande lamp naast de bank: heel geschikt om bij te lezen en eveneens voor een intieme en gezellige sfeer.

Sitúa una lámpara de pie junto al sofá: resulta muy útil para la lectura y, además, genera un ambiente íntimo y acogedor.

Posiziona una lampada a pavimento accanto al divano: è molto utile per la lettura, oltre a creare un'atmosfera intima e accogliente.

Coloque um candeeiro de pé junto ao sofá: torna-se muito útil para a leitura e, além disso, cria um ambiente íntimo e acolhedor.

Placera en golvlampa bredvid soffan; det är mycket praktiskt för läsning och skapar hemtrevlig stämning.

Place a desk behind the backrest of the sofa to save space.

Appuyer la table de travail contre le dossier du canapé permet de gagner de la place.

Bringen Sie den Schreibtisch an der Rücklehne des Sofas an, um Platz zu sparen.

Zet de werktafel tegen de achterkant van de bank om ruimte te besparen.

Apoya la mesa de trabajo sobre la parte de atrás del respaldo del sofá para ganar espacio.

Appoggia il tavolino da lavoro alla parte posteriore della spalliera del divano per guadagnare spazio.

Encoste a mesa de trabalho à parte de trás do encosto do sofá para ganhar espaço.

Placera ett arbetsbord bakom soffan för att få mer plats.

Use the space under the staircase to create a work area. Opt for a narrow desk or make it using a shelf supported on trestles.

Vous pouvez utiliser l'espace vide sous les escaliers pour créer une zone de travail : une table étroite ou tout simplement une étagère posée sur les tréteaux fera l'affaire.

Nutzen die den Platz unter der Treppe um einen Arbeitsplatz zu schaffen. Wählen Sie schmale Tische, oder errichten Sie sie mit einem Fach auf Böcken.

Gebruik de ruimte onder de trap als werkruimte. Kies voor smalle tafels of maak er zelf een met een plank op schragen.

Utiliza el hueco que queda debajo de la escalera para crear una zona de trabajo. Elige mesas estrechas o créalas con una balda apoyada sobre caballetes.

Sfrutta il vano sotto la scala per creare una zona lavoro. Opta per tavoli stretti oppure creane uno tu con una tavola appoggiata su delle capre.

Utilize o vão da escada para criar uma zona de trabalho. Escolha mesas estreitas ou crie-as com uma prateleira apoiada sobre cavaletes.

Utnyttja utrymmet under trappan för att skapa en arbetsplats. Välj ett smalt bord eller bygg ett med en hylla som läggs på träbockar.

Respect the style of the living room when building the chimney. Current trends are influenced by simple, straight lines in one color.

La cheminée doit respecter le style du salon. Les tendances actuelles présentent des formes simples, droites et d'une couleur unie.

Wenn Sie den Kamin bauen, berücksichtigen Sie den Stil des Wohnzimmers. In den aktuellen Tendenzen herrschen die einfachen, geraden, Formen und Einfarbigkeit vor.

Respecteer de stijl van de zitkamer als u een open haard wilt aanleggen. De huidige trends schrijven eenvoudige en rechte vormen met een kleur voor.

Respeta el estilo del salón a la hora de construir la chimenea. Las tendencias actuales están dominadas por las formas sencillas, rectas y de un único color.

Per realizzare il caminetto rispetta lo stile del salotto. Le tendenze attuali sono caratterizzate da forme semplici, diritte e in un unico colore.

Respeite o estilo da sala no momento de construir a lareira. As tendências actuais são dominadas pelas formas simples, direitas e de uma única cor.

Respektera vardagsrummets stil när du väljer öppen spis. Trenderna som gäller för närvarande bygger på enkla, raka former i en enda färg.

If you install a chimney in a corner you will save space in the living room.

Installer la cheminée dans un coin du salon permet d'optimiser l'espace.

Wenn Sie den Kamin in einer Ecke installieren, gewinnen Sie Platz im Wohnzimmer.

Door de open haard in een hoek te installeren creëert u meer ruimte in de zitkamer.

Si instalas la chimenea en un rincón ganarás espacio en el salón.

Se sistemi il caminetto in un angolo, guadagnerai spazio in salotto.

Se instalar a lareira num canto ganhará espaço na sala.

Om du placerar den öppna spisen i ett hörn blir det mer plats över i vardagsrummet.

Use the chimney to build a panel that partially divides the spaces.

On peut utiliser la cheminée pour construire une cloison séparant partiellement l'espace.

Nutzen Sie den Kamin um ein Paneel zu bauen, das die Räume unterteilt.

Gebruik de open haard als paneel om de ruimtes gedeeltelijk van elkaar te scheiden.

Aprovecha la chimenea para construir un panel que divida parcialmente los ambientes.

Sfrutta il caminetto per realizzare un pannello che divida parzialmente gli ambienti.

Aproveite a lareira para construir um painel que divida parcialmente os ambientes.

Utnyttja den öppna spisen för att skapa en panel som delvis skiljer områdena åt.

As an extension of the chimney, fit a built-in bench scattered with cushions. This will be one of the coziest areas in the house.

Construire une banquette en maçonnerie prolongeant la cheminée et la recouvrir de coussins permet d'obtenir l'un des lieux les plus accueillants de la maison.

Mauern Sie eine Bank als Verlängerung des Kamins, legen Sie ein paar Kissen darauf, und das Ergebnis ist einer der gemütlichsten Räume des Hauses.

Maak een gemetselde bank in het verlengde van de haard, leg er een paar kussens op; dit geeft een gezellig hoekje in het huis.

Construye un banco de obra como extensión de la chimenea, coloca unos cojines encima y tendrás como resultado uno de los espacios más acogedores de la casa.

Costruisci un piano in muratura come estensione del caminetto, sistemaci sopra dei cuscini e otterrai uno degli spazi più accoglienti della casa.

Construa um banco de alvenaria como extensão da lareira, coloque umas almofadas por cima e terá como resultado um dos espaços mais acolhedores da casa.

Bygg en inbyggd bänk som fortsättning på den öppna spisen och placera kuddar ovanpå den. Resultatet blir ett av husets mysigaste hörn.

Hanging pictures is not the only option. Rest them against
furniture, shelves or the floor and change their position
whenever you want.

Accrocher les tableaux n'est pas la seule option. Vous
pouvez les poser sur les meubles, les étagères ou le sol
et les changer de place quand vous le souhaitez.

Die Bilder aufzuhängen, ist nicht die einzige Option.
Lehnen Sie sie gegen Möbelstücke, Regale oder stellen
Sie sie auf den Boden, so können Sie sie einfach
umstellen, wann immer Sie wollen.

Schilderijen ophangen is niet de enige mogelijkheid. Laat
ze tegen meubels of planken leunen of zet ze op de grond
en verzet ze zo vaak u wilt.

Colgar los cuadros no es la única opción. Apóyalos
sobre muebles, estantes o el suelo, y cámbialos de sitio
fácilmente cuando quieras.

Appendere i quadri non è l'unica soluzione. Appoggiali
sopra mobili, ripiani o a terra; così potrai cambiarli di
posto ogni volta che vuoi.

Pendurar os quadros não é a única opção. Coloque-os
encostados aos móveis, sobre as estantes ou no chão,
e mude-os facilmente de local quando quiser.

Att hänga upp tavlorna är inte det enda alternativet. Du
kan luta dem mot möbler och hyllor eller ställa dem direkt
på golvet. Du kan lätt flytta på dem när du vill.

Use colors to define the living room in relation to other connected spaces.

Les couleurs peuvent aider à délimiter le salon par rapport aux autres espaces auxquels il est relié.

Benutzen Sie Farben, um das Wohnzimmer gegenüber den anderen Räumen, mit dem es verbunden ist, abzugrenzen.

Neem uw toevlucht tot kleuren om de zitkamer de definiëren met betrekking tot de andere ruimtes waarmee hij verbonden is.

Recurre a los colores para definir el salón respecto a los demás ambientes a los que está conectado.

Ricorri ai colori per definire il salotto rispetto agli altri ambienti a cui questo è collegato.

Recorra às cores para definir a sala em relação aos restantes espaços aos quais está ligada.

Använd färger för att skilja vardagsrummet från de intilligande rummen.

Use large cushions to create informal seating around the table in the living room.

Des coussins fermes et très volumineux deviennent des sièges informels autour de la table basse centrale du salon.

Verwenden Sie feste, dicke Kissen, um unkonventionelle Sitzgelegenheiten um den Couchtisch des Wohnzimmers herum zu gestalten.

Kies voor stevige kussens van groot formaat om informele zitplaatsen rond de salontafel van de zithoek in te richten.

Utiliza cojines firmes y de gran volumen para crear asientos informales en torno a la mesa de centro del salón.

Usa cuscini solidi e grandi per creare sedute informali intorno al tavolino centrale del salotto.

Utilize almofadas firmes e de grande volume para criar assentos informais em torno da mesa de centro da sala.

Använd stora fasta kuddar för att skapa informella sittplatser runt soffbordet.

On the walls where the heating panels are situated, place two armchairs instead of a sofa, so that the heat radiates easier in the room.

Placer des fauteuils au lieu d'un canapé contre le mur où se trouvent les radiateurs permet à la chaleur de se diffuser plus facilement.

Stellen Sie Sessel statt einem Sofa an die Wände, an denen sich die Heizkörper befinden, damit die Wärme sich leichter im Raum verbreiten kann.

Zet twee stoelen in plaats van een bank tegen de muren waar de verwarming is geïnstalleerd, zodat de warmte beter door de ruimte kan stromen.

En las paredes que soportan los paneles de la calefacción, coloca dos sillones en lugar de un sofá, para que el calor se irradie más fácilmente en el ambiente.

Sulle pareti che sostengono i pannelli per il riscaldamento, sistema due poltrne al posto di un divano affinché il calore possa irradiarsi più facilmente nell'ambiente.

Nas paredes que suportam os painéis do aquecimento, coloque duas poltronas em vez de um sofá, para que o calor se propague mais facilmente pelo ambiente.

Vid de väggar som innehåller värmepaneler kan man placera två fåtöljer istället för en soffa, så att värmen sprids bättre i hela rummet.

Move the sofa away from the wall in a diagonal position. Make use of the space created against the wall to place a designer lamp.

Vous pouvez éloigner le canapé du mur et le placer en diagonal pour utiliser l'espace créé avec la paroi et poser une lampe design.

Rücken Sie das Sofa von der Wand ab, und stellen Sie es diagonal. An den so an der Wand geschaffenen Platz stellen Sie eine Designerlampe auf.

Zet de bank schuin en iets van de muur af. Benut de verkregen ruimte bij de muur om een designlamp neer te zetten.

Aleja el sofá de la pared y sitúalo en diagonal. Aprovecha el espacio que se crea contra la pared para situar una lámpara de diseño.

Allontana il divano dalla parete e posizionalo in diagonale. Sfrutta lo spazio che si crea accanto alla parete per posizionare una lampada di design.

Afaste o sofá da parede e coloque-o na diagonal. Aproveite o espaço criado em relação à parede para colocar um candeeiro design.

Flytta soffan från väggen och placera den diagonalt. Utnyttja det utrymme som skapas mot väggen och placera en designlampa där.

The size of living room can be increased substantially if it is properly connected with the front porch through sliding doors.

Des portes coulissantes reliant directement le porche au salon permettent d'augmenter sensiblement la taille de l'espace à l'intérieur.

Das Wohnzimmer kann erheblich vergrößert werden, wenn man es durch Schiebetüren mit der Veranda verbindet.

De zitkamer lijkt aanzienlijk groter als hij op geschikte wijze doorloopt in de veranda van het huis via schuifdeuren.

El salón puede ampliar sustancialmente su tamaño si se lo comunica adecuadamente con el porche de la casa a través de puertas correderas.

Il salotto può essere ampliato in modo sostanziale se messo in comunicazione con lo spazio esterno tramite porte scorrevoli.

A sala pode ampliar substancialmente o seu tamanho caso comunique de forma adequada com o alpendre da casa através de portas de correr.

Vardagsrummets storlek kan utökas betydligt om man kopplar ihop det med husets uteplats genom skjutdörrar.

HALLS AND PASSAGEWAYS

ENTRÉES, ESCALIERS ET ZONES
DE PASSAGE

EINGANGS- UND
DURCHGANGSBEREICHE

INGANG EN LOOPRUIMTES

ENTRADAS Y ZONAS DE PASO

INGRESSO E ZONE DI PASSAGGIO

ENTRADAS E ZONAS DE PASSAGEM

ENTRÉER OCH GENOMGÅNGSOMRÅDEN

Install a decorative element to define the hall. Large or original ceiling lamps occupy very little space.

Un élément de décoration permet de délimiter l'entrée. Les lampes de plafond aux dimensions ou aux formes originales présentent l'avantage d'occuper très peu de place

Stellen Sie ein dekoratives Element auf, um den Eingangsbereich zu definieren. Die Deckenlampen in unterschiedlichen Größen und originellen Formen haben den Vorteil, dass sie sehr wenig Platz einnehmen.

Zet een decoratief element neer om de entree te definiëren. Hanglampen van grote afmetingen of met originele vormen hebben als voordeel dat ze weinig ruimte innemen.

Instala un elemento decorativo para definir el espacio de la entrada. Las lámparas de techo de dimensiones o formas originales tienen la ventaja de ocupar muy poco espacio.

Inserisci un elemento decorativo per definire lo spazio dell'ingresso. I lampadari a soffitto di dimensioni o forme originali hanno il vantaggio di occupare pochissimo spazio.

Instale um elemento decorativo para definir o espaço da entrada. Os candeeiros de tecto de dimensões ou formas originais têm a vantagem de ocupar muito pouco espaço.

Installera ett dekorativt föremål för att definiera entrén. Taklampor med originella dimensioner eller former har fördelen att de tar mycket lite plats.

In a low-ceilinged entrance, opt for light-colored cladding and furniture to create the illusion of more space.

Dans une entrée au plafond bas, il vaut mieux choisir un revêtement et des meubles clairs pour augmenter la sensation d'espace.

In einem Eingangsbereich mit niedrigen Decken sollte man für Wände und Möbel helle Farben wählen, damit der Raum größer wirkt.

In een entree met een laag plafond is het raadzaam om voor bekledingen en meubilair in lichte kleuren te kiezen, zodat de ruimte groter lijkt.

En una entrada de techos bajos conviene optar por un revestimiento y un mobiliario de tonos claros para dar sensación de mayor espacio.

In un ingresso dal soffitto basso conviene optare per rivestimenti e arredi chiari per trasmettere la sensazione di maggiore spazio

Numa entrada com tecto baixo convém optar por revestimento e mobiliário de tons claros para conferir uma sensação de espaço mais amplo.

I en entré med lågt i tak är det bäst att välja beläggning och möbler i ljusa färger för att ge intryck av större rymd.

Make use of elements of the environs to decorate halls and combine them with traditional objects such as mirrors and candelabras.

On peut utiliser les éléments de l'environnement pour décorer l'entrée, les associant à des objets traditionnels tels les glaces et les bougeoirs.

Nutzen Sie die Elemente der Umgebung um den Eingangsbereich zu dekorieren und kombinieren Sie sie mit traditionellen Gegenständen wie Spiegel und Kerzenleuchtern.

Maak gebruik van de elementen in de omgeving om de hal in te richten en combineer deze met traditionele voorwerpen zoals spiegels en kandelaars.

Aprovecha los elementos del entorno para decorar las entradas y combinarlos con objetos tradicionales como espejos y candelabros.

Sfrutta gli elementi dell'ambiente circostante per arredare l'ingresso e combinarli con oggetti tradizionali come specchi e candelabri.

Aproveite os elementos do espaço ao decorar as entradas e combine-os com objectos tradicionais como espelhos e candelabros.

Utnyttja omgivningens element för att dekorera entrén och kombinera dem med traditionella föremål som speglar och ljusstakar.

Fringed curtains are a solution to visually separate environments in a simple way without losing light. They are also very decorative.

Les rideaux frangés constituent une solution simple pour séparer visuellement les espaces sans renoncer à la lumière. De plus, ils sont très décoratifs.

Die Fransengardine ist eine gute Lösung, um die Bereiche ohne Lichtverlust optische voneinander zu trennen. Außerdem sind sie sehr dekorativ.

Gordijnen met gerafelde randen vormen een oplossing om de ruimtes visueel van elkaar te scheiden, zonder dat ze licht wegnemen. Ze zijn bovendien erg decoratief.

La cortina de flecos es una solución para separar visualmente los ambientes de una manera sencilla y sin perder luz. Además, son muy decorativas.

La tenda di frange è una soluzione per dividere visivamente gli ambienti in modo semplice senza rinunciare alla luce, oltre a essere molto decorativa.

A cortina de franjas é uma solução para separar visualmente os espaços de uma forma simples e sem perder luz. Além disso, são muito decorativas.

Ett draperi är en lösning för att visuellt skilja olika utrymmen åt på ett enkelt sätt utan att förlora ljus. Dessutom är det mycket dekorativt.

Place a small bright-colored chair in the hall, but avoid turning it into a makeshift coat rack on which the coats are thrown upon entering the house.

Ce petit fauteuil d'une couleur vive égaye l'entrée. Il faut toutefois éviter qu'il ne se transforme en un portemanteau improvisé où l'on accroche les vêtements dès qu'on accède à la maison.

Stellen Sie einen kleinen Sessel in einer attraktiven Farbe in den Eingangsbereich, aber vermeiden Sie, dass er als improvisierter Kleiderständer benutzt wird, auf den alle Mäntel geworfen werden, sobald man das Haus betritt.

Zet een kleine fauteuil in een aantrekkelijke kleur bij de ingang, maar zorg ervoor dat deze niet verandert in geïmproviseerde kapstok waar men bij binnenkomst meteen de jas op gooit.

Coloca un pequeño sillón de color atractivo en la entrada, pero evita convertirlo en un perchero improvisado en el que se tiran los abrigos apenas se entra en la vivienda.

Sistema una poltroncina dal colore vivace all'ingresso, ma evita di trasformarla in un appendiabiti improvvisato dove chi entra in casa appoggia giacche e cappotti.

Coloque uma pequena poltrona de cor atractiva à entrada, mas evite convertê-la num cabide improvisado no qual se colocam os casacos logo que se entra na habitação.

Placera en liten fåtölj i en attraktiv färg i entrén, men undvik att förvandla den till en improviserad klädhängare där man slänger jackor så fort man kommer innanför dörren.

A pair of shelves, a table, a mirror and striking wallpaper are enough to create an original and, above all, a very practical entrance hall.

Quelques étagères, une petite table, un miroir et du papier peint haut en couleur suffisent à créer une entrée originale et surtout très pratique.

Ein paar Regalbretter, ein Tischchen, ein Spiegel und eine auffallende Tapete sind ausreichend für einen originellen und vor allem sehr praktischen Empfangsbereich.

Een paar planken, een tafeltje, een spiegel en een opvallende muur zijn voldoende om en originele en vooral zeer praktische hal te verkrijgen.

Un par de baldas, una mesilla, un espejo y un papel de pared llamativo son suficientes para crear un recibidor original y sobre todo muy práctico.

Un paio di mensole, un tavolino, uno specchio e una vivace carta da parati bastano per creare un ingresso originale e soprattutto molto pratico.

Um par de prateleiras, uma mesa-de-cabeceira, um espelho e um papel de parede chamativo são suficientes para criar um hall original e sobretudo muito prático.

Ett par hyllor, ett litet bord, en spegel och en originell tapet är det enda som krävs för att skapa en originell och praktisk hall.

Install a built-in book shelf on the wall bordering the front door to place ornaments, boxes to hold keys, letter trays, lamps, etc.

Sur des étagères en maçonnerie bâties sur la paroi jouxtant la porte d'entrée, on peut placer des objets de décoration, des petites boites à clés, des bacs à courrier, des lampes, etc.

Bauen Sie ein paar Regale in die Wand neben der Eingangstür für Ziergegenstände, Schlüsselkästchen, Fächer für die Post, Lampen, usw., ein.

Enkele gemetselde planken aan de muur die grenst aan de voordeur zijn een manier om versieringen, doosjes voor sleutels, bakjes voor de correspondentie, lampen, etc. neer te zetten.

Coloca unos estantes de obra en la pared lindante a la puerta de entrada para instalar adornos, cajitas para guardar las llaves, bandejas para la correspondencia, lámparas, etc.

Sistema dei ripiani in muratura sulla parete che confina con la porta di ingresso su cui poggiare soprammobili, scatole per le chiavi, vassoi per la corrispondenza, punti luce, ecc.

Aplique umas estantes de alvenaria na parede contígua à porta de entrada para colocar adornos, caixas para guardar as chaves, bandejas para a correspondência, candeeiros, etc.

Placera inbyggda hyllor på väggen närmast ingången för prydnadsföremål, askar för nycklarna, brickor för post, lampor etc.

Cantilevered staircases are visually very lightweight and therefore ideal for small environments. The colored steps that contrast with the wall become decorative elements.

Visuellement très légers, les escaliers à encorbellement sont adaptés à des espaces réduits. Les marches d'une couleur qui contrastent avec les murs se transforment en éléments de décoration.

Auskragende Treppen wirken sehr leicht und sind daher für kleine Räume geeignet. Stufen, deren Farbe mit der Wand kontrastiert, werden zu dekorativen Elementen.

Zwevende trappen zien er heel licht uit en zijn daarom ideaal voor kleine ruimtes. De kleurige traptreden contrasteren met de muur en veranderen daardoor in decoratieve elementen.

Las escaleras en voladizo son visualmente muy livianas y, por tanto, idóneas para ambientes pequeños. Los peldaños de color que contrastan con la pared se convierten en elementos decorativos.

Le scale aperte sono visivamente molto leggere e quindi adatte ad ambienti di piccole dimensioni. I gradini realizzati in colori contrastanti con la parete si trasformano in elementi decorativi.

As escadas em suspensão são visualmente muito leves e, portanto, ideais para ambientes pequenos. Os degraus coloridos de forma a contrastarem com a parede convertem-se em elementos decorativos.

Rundade trappor är visuellt mycket lätta och därför idealiska för små utrymmen. Trappsteg i färger som kontrasterar mot väggen bildar dekorativa element.

Give the staircase a special touch with a striking piece of furniture on the landing, whether it is a chair, a small but high table or a lamp.

Vous pouvez donner à votre escalier une touche spéciale, en décorant le palier avec un meuble design attrayant – un fauteuil, une petite table haute ou une lampe.

Geben Sie der Treppe mit einem auffallenden Möbelstück auf dem Absatz, entweder ein Sessel, ein kleiner aber hoher Tisch oder eine Lampe eine besondere Note.

Geef de trap een speciaal accent met een meubelstuk met opvallend ontwerp op de overloop, of kies voor een leunstoel, een klein, maar hoog tafeltje of een lamp.

Confiere a la escalera un toque especial con un mueble de diseño llamativo en el descansillo, ya sea un sillón, una mesita pequeña pero alta o una lámpara.

Per dare un tocco speciale alla scala, inserisci a metà rampa un arredo di design che catturi l'attenzione; andrà bene una poltrona, un tavolino piccolo ma alto, oppure un punto luce.

Confira à escada um toque especial com um móvel de design atraente no patamar, seja uma poltrona, uma mesa pequena mas alta ou um candeeiro.

Ge trappan speciell karaktär med en uppseendeväckande designmöbel i hallen. Det kan vara en fåtölj, ett litet, högt bord eller en lampa.

Staircases in passageways or in bright rooms should have transparent, thick acrylic or glass handrails to let light through and to integrate better into the room.

Les escaliers situés dans les lieux de passage ou dans les pièces très lumineuses devraient être équipés de balustrades transparentes, en acrylique ou en verre très épais, pour laisser passer la lumière et pour mieux s'intégrer à l'espace environnant.

Treppen in sehr hellen Durchgangsbereichen oder Zimmern sollten durchsichtige Geländer aus Acryl oder sehr dickem Glas haben, damit sie das Licht durchlassen und sich besser in den Raum einfügen.

Trappen in loopruimtes of zeer lichte kamers moeten heel dikke, doorschijnende leuningen - van acryl of glas - hebben, om het licht door te laten en beter te integreren in de ruimte.

Las escaleras en zonas de paso o en habitaciones muy luminosas deberían llevar barandillas transparentes (de acrílico o cristal muy grueso) para dejar pasar la luz e integrarse mejor en el ambiente.

Le scale nelle zone di passaggio o nelle stanze molto luminose dovrebbero essere dotate di protezioni trasparenti in materiale acrilico o vetro molto spesso che consenta il passaggio della luce e si integri meglio nell'ambiente.

As escadas em zonas de passagem ou em quartos com muita luz deverão conter varandins transparentes de acrílico ou vidro muito espesso para que deixem passar a luz e se integrem melhor no ambiente.

Trappor i genomgångsområden eller mycket ljusa rum bör ha genomskinliga handräcken av mycket tjock akryl eller glas så att ljuset släpps igenom och den smälter in bättre i miljön.

In environments with a mezzanine, put a ladder against the wall so as not to obstruct traffic. In this way it is stronger and safer.

Dans une pièce avec mezzanine, l'escalier peut être collé contre le mur pour éviter qu'il ne gêne la circulation, ce qui par ailleurs le rend aussi plus stable et plus sûr.

In Räumen mit Zwischengeschoss bringen Sie die Treppe an der Wand an, damit die Zirkulation nicht behindert wird. Außerdem ist sie so stärker und sicherer.

Plaats, in ruimtes met een tussenverdieping, de trap tegen de muur zodat deze geen sta-in-de-weg wordt. Dit is bovendien steviger en veiliger.

En los ambientes con entresuelo, sitúa la escalera contra la pared para que no entorpezca la circulación. Además, así es más firme y segura.

Negli ambienti con mezzanino, è meglio posizionare la scala contro la parete affinché non ostacoli il passaggio. In tal modo sarà anche più solida e sicura.

Em espaços com sobreloja, coloque a escada contra a parede para que não atrapalhe a circulação. Além disso, a estrutura também será mais firme e segura.

I rum med halvtrapor kan man placera trappan mot väggen så att den inte är i väggen. Dessutom är det mer stabilt och säkert.

Stairwells offer numerous possibilities of use. A built-in bookshelf some 11 inches off the floor can be used as shelf, seat and storage.

Les escaliers offrent des espaces vides qui se prêtent à des usages multiples. Une bibliothèque en maçonnerie construite à 30 cm du sol devient une surface d'appoint, une banquette et un lieu de rangement.

Der Platz unter der Treppe bietet vielfältige Verwendungsmöglichkeiten. Ein in 30 cm Höhe eingebautes Bord fungiert als Regal, Sitzplatz und Stauraum.

De ruimte onder de trap biedt talrijke gebruiksmogelijkheden. Een gemetselde rand op 30 cm van de grond kan dienst doen als plank, zitplaats en opbergruimte.

Los huecos de la escalera ofrecen numerosas posibilidades de uso. Un estante de obra a 30 cm del suelo funciona como balda, asiento y distribuidor de almacenaje.

I vani scala offrono numerose possibilità di utilizzo. Un ripiano in muratura posto a 30 cm da terra può servire come mensola, seduta o essere utilizzato per riporre gli oggetti in modo organizzato.

Os vãos da escada oferecem numerosas possibilidades de uso. Uma estante de alvenaria a 30 cm do solo funciona como prateleira, banco e organizador para arrumação.

Utrymmet under trapporna har många användningsmöjligheter. En inbyggd hylla 30 cm från golvet fungerar som hylla, sittplats och förvaring.

When constructing a staircase, take into account the required slope and the measurement ratio of the steps so that they are easy to climb.

Lors de la construction d'un escalier, pour qu'il soit facile à monter, il faut que l'inclinaison soit correcte et les dimensions des marches proportionnées.

Beim Bau der Treppe berücksichtigen Sie die angemessene Neigung und die entsprechende Höhe der Stufen, damit man bequem hinaufgehen kann.

Houd bij het bouwen van de trap rekening met de geschikte klimlijn en de proportie van de afmetingen van de treden, zodat hij eenvoudig te beklimmen is.

A la hora de construir una escalera ten en cuenta la inclinación apropiada y la proporción de las medidas de los peldaños para que sea fácil subirla.

Nella realizzazione di una scala occorre tenere conto dell'inclinazione e delle proporzioni dei gradini affinché sia facile salire.

No momento de construir uma escada é necessário ter em conta a inclinação apropriada e a proporção das medidas dos degraus para que seja fácil subir.

När man bygger en trappa bör man tänka på att den ska ha den rätta lutningen och proportionen på trappstegens mått så att den är lätt att gå på.

Ceiling lights on the landings must be dynamic when the stairs are very long. In this way, they also serve as a visual break.

Si l''escalier est très large, la lampe de plafond décorant le palier doit être marquante. Elle servira ainsi de pause visuelle.

Wenn die Treppen sehr hoch sind, müssen die Deckenlampen über den Treppenabsätzen groß genug sein. Dadurch wirken sie zudem als visueller Ruhepunkt.

Plafondlampen in de overloop moeten overtuigend zijn als de trap heel lang is. Op deze manier doen ze ook dienst als visueel rustpunt.

Las lámparas de techo en los descansillos deben ser contundentes cuando las escaleras son muy largas. De esta manera funcionan además como un descanso visual.

I lampadari a soffitto nei disimpegni devono essere di forte impatto visivo quando le scale sono molto lunghe. In tal modo serviranno anche come punto di "riposo visivo".

Os candeeiros de tecto nos patamares devem ser eficazes quando as escadas são muito longas. Desta forma funcionam também como um descanso visual.

Om trappan är mycket lång bör taklamporna i hallen vara väl tilltagna. På så sätt fungerar de också som ett visuellt viloelement.

If the stairs are narrow and dark, paint the side walls white to create a feeling of spaciousness.

Si l'escalier est étroit et réalisé avec des matériaux sombres, il vaut mieux peindre les murs latéraux en blanc pour augmenter la sensation d'espace.

Wenn die Treppen schmal sind und aus dunklem Material bestehen, streichen Sie die Seitenwände weiß, um einen Eindruck von Weite zu vermitteln.

Verf, als de trap smal is en donker van kleur de zijwanden wit, zodat het geheel ruimer lijkt.

Siempre que las escaleras sean angostas y, además, de materiales oscuros, pinta las paredes laterales de color blanco para dar sensación de amplitud.

Se le scale sono anguste e realizzate in materiali scuri, conviene dipingere le pareti laterali di bianco per trasmettere una sensazione di maggiore ampiezza.

Sempre que as escadas sejam estreitas e construídas com materiais escuros, pinte as paredes laterais na cor branca para conferir uma sensação de amplitude.

Om trappan är smal och av mörka material bör man måla väggarna vita, för att skapa en känsla av rymd.

Improve safety on the stairs with spotlights on the roof, side panels and wall sconces. Install switches at the bottom and top of the staircase to be able to turn on and off the light from either point.

La sécurité de votre escalier est renforcée par un éclairage au plafond, au niveau des marches ou latéral, ainsi que des appliques murales. Les interrupteurs situés au début et à la fin de la structure permettent d'allumer ou d'éteindre la lumière en toute sécurité.

Erhöhen Sie die Sicherheit auf der Treppe durch in die Decke, in die Stufen oder seitlich eingebaute Strahler oder Wandlampen. Installieren Sie am Fuß und am Ende der Treppe Schalter, damit man das Licht an den jeweiligen Orten ein- und ausschalten kann.

Vergroot de veiligheid in de trap met in het plafond, traptreden of zijwanden ingebouwde spots en wandlampen. Installeer schakelaars onder en bovenaan de trap, zodat het licht op ieder moment kan worden aan en uitgedaan.

Potencia la seguridad en la escalera con focos empotrados en el techo, peldaños o laterales y apliques de pared. Instala interruptores en el comienzo y el final de la escalera para poder encender y apagar la luz desde cualquier punto.

Aumenta la sicurezza della scala con punti luce incassati nel soffitto, nei gradini o sulle fasce laterali, oltre ad applique sulle pareti. Inserisci degli interruttori alla base e in cima alla scala per poter accendere e spegnere la luce da qualsiasi punto

Reforce a segurança na escada com focos embutidos no tecto, nos degraus ou nas laterais e candeeiros de parede. Instale interruptores no início e no fim da escada para poder ligar e desligar a luz a partir de qualquer ponto.

Förstärk säkerheten i trappan med infällda spotlights i taket, på trappstegen eller på sidorna, och väggbelysning. Placera strömbrytate i början och slutet av trappan för att kunna tända och släcka lamporna från flera olika platser.

Single flight staircases can be located in the center of the room to contribute to the layout of the space.

L'escalier droit à une seule volée peut occuper le centre du salon, contribuant ainsi à distribuer l'espace environnant.

Eine einläufige, gerade Treppe kann in der Mitte des Wohnzimmers errichtet werden und als Raumteiler dienen.

Een trap met een rechte traparm moet in het midden van de zitkamer worden geplaatst, om bij te dragen aan de indeling van deze ruimte.

La escalera de un único tramo recto puede situarse en el centro del salón para contribuir a la distribución de ese ambiente.

La scala in un unico elemento retto può essere posizionata al centro del salotto, contribuendo così alla distribuzione dell'ambiente.

A escada com uma única secção recta pode ser situada no centro da sala para contribuir para a distribuição desse espaço.

En trappa som är i ett rakt stycke kan placeras i mitten av vardagsrummet för att bidra till rummets distribution.

Slightly reduce the width of the stairs and make use of the side against the wall to mount a shelf.

Réduisant légèrement la largeur de l'escalier, on obtient un espace latéral accolé au mur où l'on peut installer des étagères.

Machen Sie die Treppe etwas schmaler und stellen Sie an der Wandseite ein Regal auf.

Maak de trap iets minder breed en benut de zijkant tegen de muur om een boekenkast te monteren.

Reduce un poco el ancho de la escalera y aprovecha el lateral contra la pared para montar una estantería.

Riduci leggermente l'ampiezza della scala e sfrutta il lato a parete per montarvi una serie di ripiani.

Reduza um pouco a largura da escada e aproveite a lateral que acompanha a parede para montar estantes.

Förminska trappans bredd något och utnyttja sidan mot väggen för att bygga en hylla.

A cantilever spiral staircase is a great way to save space. It also adds a sculptural element to the space.

L'escalier hélicoïdal à encorbellement constitue une excellente manière d'optimiser l'espace. Par ailleurs, il ajoute un élément sculptural à l'environnement.

Eine Wendeltreppe ist eine ausgezeichnete Lösung, um Platz zu gewinnen. Außerdem bringt sie ein gestalterisches Element in den Raum.

Een zwevende wenteltrap is een uitstekende manier om ruimte te besparen. Het voegt bovendien een beeldhouw-element toe aan de ruimte.

Una escalera de caracol volada es una excelente manera de ganar espacio. Además, agrega un elemento escultórico al ambiente.

Una scala a chiocciola sospesa è un'ottimo modo per guadagnare spazio. Aggiunge inoltre un tocco scultoreo all'ambiente

Uma escada suspensa em caracol é uma excelente forma de ganhar espaço. Além disso, acrescenta um elemento escultural ao espaço.

En fristående spiraltrappa är ett utmärkt sätt att utnyttja utrymmet. Dessutom fungerar det som ett skulpturellt bidrag till rummet.

Corridors with skylights are ideal to place large plants. These potted ficus tree in large pots add a green touch to the house.

Les couloirs avec verrière au plafond sont parfaits pour accueillir des plantes de grandes dimensions. Ces ficus en pots géants apportent une note verte à la maison.

Flure mit Oberlicht sind ideal für die Aufstellung großer Pflanzen. Diese eingetopften Ficus-Bäume der Größe XXL bringen eine *green* Atmosphäre ins Haus.

Gangen met dakramen zijn ideaal om grote planten neer te zetten. Deze ficussen in XXL-formaat bloembakken geven de woning tevens een *groen* accent.

Los pasillos con tragaluz son ideales para situar plantas de gran formato. Estos árboles de ficus en macetas de tamaño XXL aportan un aire *green* a la casa.

I corridoi con lucernario sono ideali per sistemarvi piante di grandi dimensioni. Questi ficus extra-large contribuiscono con aria *green* al benessere della casa.

Os corredores com clarabóia são ideais para colocar plantas com grandes dimensões. Estas figueiras em vasos de tamanho XXL conferem um ar *green* à casa.

Korridorer med takfönster är idealiska platser för stora krukväxter. Dessa fikusar i extra stora krukor ger en *grön* känsla åt huset.

The staircase landing is not the only place you can hang a large format lamp. Place it in the middle of the slope at a height that does not get in the way.

Le palier de l'escalier n'est pas le seul endroit où l'on peut accrocher un lustre de grand format. Il peut être placé au centre de la pente à une hauteur qui ne gêne pas la circulation.

Der Treppenabsatz ist nicht der einzige Ort, an dem man eine großformatige Lampe aufhängen kann. Hängen Sie die Lampe in die Mitte der Neigung in einer Höhe, die die Zirkulation nicht behindert.

De overloop van de trap is niet de enige plaats waar een grote lamp kan worden opgehangen. Plaats deze halverwege de trap op een hoogte waardoor de doorgang niet belemmerd wordt.

El descansillo de la escalera no es el único sitio del que puede colgar una lámpara de gran formato. Sitúa esta en medio de la pendiente a una altura que no afecte la circulación.

Il pianerottolo di una scala non è l'unico punto in cui è possibile sistemare un lampadario di grandi dimensioni. Posizionala a metà della diagonale, a un'altezza che non intralci il passaggio.

O patamar da escada não é o único onde é possível suspender um candeeiro de grande dimensão. Coloque este a meio da inclinação a uma altura que não perturbe a circulação.

Trapphuset är inte det enda stället där man kan placera en lampa i stort format. Placera den på en höjd som inte påverkar trafiken.

Make use of outdoor passageways to put up a hammock and create a special corner in the courtyard.

Vous pouvez utiliser les couloirs extérieurs pour accrocher un hamac et créer ainsi un coin spécial dans la cour de la maison.

Nutzen Sie die äußeren Korridore um eine Hängematte anzubringen und im Patio des Hauses eine besondere Nische zu schaffen.

Gebruik de gangen buiten om een schommelbank te plaatsen en creëer zo een bijzonder plekje in de patio van de woning.

Aprovecha los pasillos exteriores para instalar una hamaca colgante y crear un rincón especial en el patio de la casa.

Sfrutta i corridoi esterni per appendere un'amaca e creare un angolo speciale nel patio di casa.

Aproveite os corredores exteriores para instalar uma cama suspensa e criar um espaço especial no pátio da casa.

Använd de yttre gångarna på huset för att placera en enorm hängmatta och skapa en speciell plats på husets gård.

Pictures help to make a transition wall between two rooms in the house stand out and can even connect the style of the spaces.

Les tableaux contribuent à mettre en valeur une cloison de transition entre deux espaces et permettent aussi de relier les différents styles de la maison.

Bilder tragen dazu bei, eine Wand zwischen zwei Bereichen des Hauses hervorzuheben, und können sogar den Stil der beiden Bereiche verbinden.

Schilderijen kunnen meehelpen om een muur die een overgang vormt tussen twee ruimtes van de woning te accentueren en kunnen zelfs de stijl van de ruimtes met elkaar verbinden.

Los cuadros contribuyen a destacar una pared de transición entre dos espacios de la casa e incluso pueden conectar el estilo de los ambientes.

I quadri contribuiscono a dare risalto a una parete di transizione tra due spazi della casa e possono persino richiamare lo stile degli ambienti.

Os quadros contribuem para fazer sobressair uma parede de transição entre dois espaços da casa e podem inclusivamente ligar o estilo dos ambientes.

Tavlor hjälper till att framhäva en genomgångsvägg mellan två rum i huset och kan även sammanlänka stilen på två olika platser.

The corridor leading to the bedroom can accommodate a wardrobe, hidden behind curtains that are both decorative and functional.

Le couloir conduisant à la chambre à coucher peut abriter une penderie ou un dressing, cachés derrière des rideaux aussi bien fonctionnels que décoratifs.

Op de gang naar een kamer kan een kledingkast worden neergezet, verborgen achter een gordijn dat, behalve functioneel, ook decoratief is.

Im Flur, der zum Schlafzimmer führt, kann ein Kleiderschrank stehen, der hinter Vorhängen versteckt ist, die nicht nur nützlich, sondern auch dekorativ sind.

El pasillo que conduce a la habitación puede albergar un armario para la ropa, escondido detrás de unas cortinas, que, además de funcionales, resultan decorativas.

Il corridoio che porta alla stanza può ospitare un armadio per i vestiti, nascosto dietro delle tende, funzionali e decorative.

O corredor que conduz ao quarto pode albergar um armário para a roupa, escondido atrás de umas cortinas que além de funcionais também se tornam decorativas.

Hallen som leder till sovrummet kan ge plats åt en garderob, som döljs bakom gardiner som är både funktionella och dekorativa.

Use a setback in the wall of the corridor to create a built-in sofa.

Vous pouvez profiter d'un décrochement dans le mur du couloir pour construire un canapé en maçonnerie.

Nutzen Sie eine Nische in der Flurwand, um ein Sofa einzubauen.

Benut een terugspringing in de muur van de gang om een gemetselde bank te maken.

Aprovecha un retranqueo en la pared del pasillo para hacer un sofá de obra.

Sfrutta un rientro della parete del corridoio per realizzare un divano in muratura.

Aproveite uma reentrância na parede do corredor para fazer um sofá de alvenaria.

Utnyttja en fördjupning i hallväggen för att göra en inbyggd soffa.

Combine built-in step with other pieces of carpentry work
and use them as drawers.

Les marches en maçonnerie alternées aux marches
en bois deviennent des tiroirs.

Kombinieren Sie eingebaute Stufen mit getischlerten
Fächern und verwenden Sie sie als Schubfächer.

Combineer gemetselde en houten traptreden en benut
deze laatste als laden.

Combina peldaños de obra con otros de carpintería
y aprovéchalos como cajones.

Combina i gradini in muratura con altri in legno e utilizzali
come cassetti.

Combine degraus de alvenaria com elementos
de carpintaria e aproveite-os como gavetas.

Kombinera inbyggda steg med andra snickrade och
använd dem som lådor.

KITCHEN
CUISINE
KÜCHE
KEUKEN
COCINA
CUCINA
COZINHA
KÖKET

If you enjoy cooking, install a fireplace for roasting and baking bread and pizza. It does not need to be a large space, just a good connection with the exterior.

Si vous aimez cuisiner, vous pouvez installer une cheminée pour cuire votre pain et vos pizzas. Vous n'avez pas besoin de beaucoup d'espace, juste d'un bon lien avec l'extérieur.

Wenn Sie gerne kochen, bauen Sie einen Kaminofen zum Backen von Brot und Pizza ein. Man braucht keinen großen Raum, nur eine gute Verbindung nach draußen.

Houdt u van koken, installeer dan een vuurhaard om brood en pizza in te bakken. Er is niet veel ruimte nodig, alleen een goede verbinding naar buiten toe.

Si disfrutas cocinando, instala una chimenea para asar y hornear pan y *pizza*. No se necesita un espacio muy grande, sólo una buena conexión del ambiente con el exterior.

Se ti piace cucinare, installa un caminetto per fare arrosti, pane e pizza. Non serve molto spazio, basta un buon collegamento tra la stanza e l'esterno.

Se gosta de cozinhar, instale um grelhador para assar e cozer pão e piza. Não é necessária uma área muito grande, apenas uma boa ligação do espaço interior com o exterior.

Om du tycker om att laga mat kan du installera en ugn för att grilla och baka bröd och pizza. Det behövs inte mycket plats, bara en bra utomhusanslutning.

Put appliances like the oven and the microwave on top of each other, located at the right height, to save space and convenience when working with them.

On peut superposer les éléments d'électroménagers, tels le four et le micro-ondes, à bonne hauteur, pour gagner de l'espace et qu'ils soient pratiques à utiliser.

Bringen Sie Haushaltsgeräte wie Ofen und Mikrowelle übereinander in einer angemessenen Höhe an, um Platz zu gewinnen und bequem mit ihnen arbeiten zu können.

Plaats huishoudelijke apparaten zoals de oven en de magnetron in een toren, op een geschikte hoogte, voor meer ruimte en comfort tijdens het koken.

Coloca los electrodomésticos como el horno y el microondas en torre, situados a la altura adecuada, para ganar espacio y comodidad a la hora de trabajar con ellos.

Sistema gli elettrodomestici come il forno e il microonde uno sopra l'altro, a un'altezza adeguata, per guadagnare spazio e comfort durante il loro utilizzo.

Coloque os electrodomésticos como o forno e o microondas em torre, situados à altura adequada, para ganhar espaço e comodidade no momento de trabalhar com eles.

Placera vitvaror som ugn och mikrovågsugn i ett torn, på lämplig höjd. På så sätt får du mer plats och det är bekvämare när man ska arbeta med dem.

Opt for furniture with deep drawers and organizers that leave everything that you need in sight.

Vous pouvez choisir des meubles avec des tiroirs profonds et des rangements qui laissent voir tout ce dont vous avez besoin.

Entscheiden Sie sich für Schränke mit tiefen unterteilten Schubladen, in denen alles, was man braucht, sichtbar ist.

Kies voor meubels met diepe laden met verdeelvakken zodat alle benodigdheden in een oogopslag zichtbaar zijn.

Decántate por muebles con cajones profundos con organizadores que dejan a la vista todo lo que se necesita.

Opta per mobili con cassetti profondi e divisori per renderne visibile il contenuto.

Opte por móveis com gavetas profundas e organizadores que deixem à vista tudo o que é necessário.

Välj möbler med djupa lådor med förvaringsfack som gör det lätt att se allt du behöver.

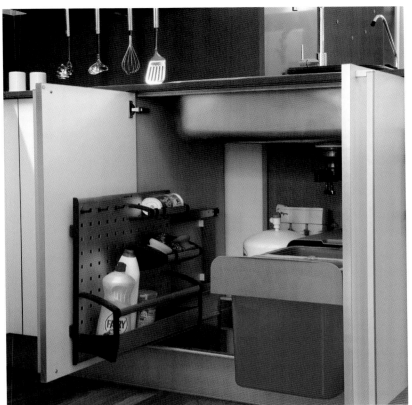

A waste area below the worktop clears the work area more easily. Make use of the same space to organize cleaning products in a rack attached to the cupboard door.

Un espace réservé aux déchets sous le plan de travail permet de le débarrasser plus facilement. On peut profiter de cette partie pour ranger les produits d'entretien dans un support monté contre la porte du meuble.

Ein Bereich für die Abfälle unter der Arbeitsplatte erleichtert das Aufräumen des Arbeitsbereichs. Nutzen Sie denselben Platz, um die Putzmittel an einer an der Schranktür angebrachten Platte unterzubringen.

Afvalbakken onder het aanrecht zorgen ervoor dat de werkruimte gemakkelijk kan worden opgeruimd. Benut dezelfde plaats om schoonmaakmiddelen op te bergen in een rekje dat aan de kastdeur is bevestigd.

Una zona para los residuos debajo de la encimera despeja más fácilmente el área de trabajo. Aprovecha el mismo espacio para organizar los productos de limpieza en una plancha adosada a la puerta del armario.

Una zona per i rifiuti sotto il ripiano consente di pulire più facilmente l'area di lavoro. Sfrutta questo spazio anche per sistemare i prodotti per la pulizia, attaccando un ripiano allo sportello del mobile.

Uma zona para os resíduos sob a bancada liberta mais facilmente a área de trabalho. Aproveite o mesmo espaço para organizar os produtos de limpeza num suporte fixo à porta do armário.

E plats för avfall under diskbänken håller arbetsbänken fri. Använda samma plats för att organisera dina städartiklar i ett inbyggt fack i skåpets dörr.

Make use of empty spaces in the wall and mount a shelf for the dishes and glasses.

Les espaces vides du mur sont destinés aux étagères pour la vaisselle et les verres.

Nutzen Sie die freien Wandflächen und installieren Sie ein Regal für das Geschirr und die Gläser.

Benut lege ruimtes aan de muur en monteer een wandmeubel voor serviesgoed en glazen.

Aprovecha los espacios vacíos en la pared y monta una estantería para la vajilla y los vasos.

Sfrutta gli spazi vuoti sulla parete e monta uno scaffale per piatti e bicchieri.

Aproveite os espaços vazios na parede e monte estantes para a louça e para os copos.

Utnyttja de tomma ytorna på väggen och sätt upp en hylla för porslin och glas.

Save time by having items you use daily at hand. If they are classified by color or size, order is guaranteed.

Avoir les objets à usage quotidien à portée de la main fait gagner du temps. Le classement par couleur ou par dimension assure un rangement très réussi.

Die Dinge des täglichen Gebrauchs bei der Hand zu haben spart Zeit; wenn sie außerdem nach Farben oder Größe geordnet sind, ist der Eindruck von Ordnung garantiert.

Zorg dat u de voorwerpen die u dagelijks gebruikt bij de hand heeft; als u ze ook nog op kleur of maat sorteert ziet het er bovendien geordend uit.

Tener a mano los objetos de uso diario te permitirá ahorrar tiempo; si además están clasificados por colores o tamaños, el efecto de orden está garantizado.

Avere a portata di mano gli oggetti di uso quotidiano ti consentirà di risparmiare tempo; se poi sono classificati per colore o dimensioni, l'effetto di ordine è garantito!

Ter à mão os objectos de uso diário permitirá poupar tempo; se além disso estiverem classificados por cores ou tamanhos o efeito de ordem está assegurado.

Att ha de mest använda föremålen till hands sparar tid, och om du dessutom klassificerar dem efter färg eller storlek kommer det garanterat att vara ordning.

To create order on open shelves group objects by shape or color. Inside cupboards the distribution of household goods does not have to be so fussy.

Les étagères ouvertes exigent que les objets soient rangés par forme ou par couleur pour donner la sensation d'ordre. Les ustensiles les moins attrayants sont distribués à l'intérieur des meubles.

Offene Regale machen es erforderlich, dass die Gegenstände nach ähnlichen Formen oder Farben geordnet sind, um aufgeräumt zu wirken. Bringen sie die am wenigsten attraktiven Haushaltsgegenstände in den Schränken unter.

Voor niet afgesloten wandmeubels moeten de voorwerpen op vorm of per kleur zijn gerangschikt, zodat het er opgeruimd uit ziet. Zet minder aantrekkelijke huisraad in de kasten.

Los estantes abiertos requieren que los objetos estén agrupados por formas aproximadas o colores, para dar sensación de orden. Distribuye el menaje menos atractivo en el interior de los armarios.

Per trasmettere la sensazione di ordine, i ripiani aperti devono contenere oggetti raggruppati per forme simili o per colore. Sistema gli articoli meno attraenti all'interno dei pensili.

As estantes abertas requerem que os objectos estejam agrupados por formas aproximadas ou cores, para dar a sensação de ordem. Distribua os elementos menos atractivos no interior dos armários.

Öppna hyllor kräver att föremålen är indelade efter liknande former eller färger, för att ge intryck av ordning. Placera de minst attraktiva husgeråden inne i skåpen.

If you have the space and a square-shaped kitchen, incorporate a kitchen island: it gives you extra working space and storage.

Si vous disposez d'un espace cuisine carré, vous pouvez en profiter pour intégrer un îlot indépendant, qui augmente la surface du plan de travail et l'espace de rangement.

Wenn Sie Platz haben und die Küche einen quadratischen Grundriss hat, bauen Sie eine unabhängige Kochinsel ein: Dadurch gewinnen Sie einen zusätzlichen Arbeits- und Aufbewahrungsplatz.

Heeft u voldoende ruimte en een keuken met vierkant oppervlak, aarzel dan niet om een onafhankelijk kookeiland te installeren: zo heeft u een groter werkoppervlak en meer opbergruimte.

Si cuentas con espacio y una planta de cocina cuadrada, no dudes en integrar una isla independiente: suma superficie extra de trabajo y almacenaje.

Se hai spazio e una cucina a pianta quadrata, opta per l'aggiunta di un'isola centrale: aggiungerà superficie di lavoro e contenimento.

Caso disponha de espaço e uma planta de cozinha quadrada, não hesite em integrar uma ilha independente: uma superfície extra de trabalho e arrumação.

Om du har plats och om ditt kök är fyrkantigt så tveka inte att installera en köksö: det ger extra arbetsytor och förvaringsutrymme.

Go for an island with a breakfast bar seating area so the family can gather in the kitchen while you are preparing the meal.

Les îlots avec bar permettent de prendre des repas rapides. La famille peut aussi se réunir dans la cuisine pendant la préparation des plats.

Wählen Sie eine Kochinsel mit Theke für Schnellmahlzeiten oder damit sich die Familie in der Küche versammeln kann, während Sie das Essen zubereiten.

Kies voor eilanden met bars voor een snelle maaltijd of als plaats waar het gezin bij elkaar kan zitten tijdens het bereiden van de maaltijd.

Apuesta por las islas con barras para comidas rápidas o para que la familia se reúna en la cocina mientras preparas la comida.

Le isole con bancone sono ideali per i pasti veloci o per riunire la famiglia in cucina durante la preparazione dei pasti.

Opte por ilhas com balcão para poder fazer refeições rápidas ou para que a família se reúna na cozinha enquanto prepara a comida.

Satsa på en köksö med bardisk för snabba måltider och för att familjen ska kunna samlas medans man lagar maten.

Replace one of the narrow drawers with a shelf that can serve as a working space.

Les petits tiroirs peuvent être remplacés par une planche coulissante faisant office de table d'appoint.

Ersetzten Sie eine der schmalen Schubladen durch eine ausziehbare Platte, die als Beistelltisch dient.

Vervang een of meerdere smalle laden door een uittrekbare plank die dienst kan doen als bijzettafel.

Sustituye uno de los cajones angostos por una balda extraíble que funciona como mesa auxiliar.

Sostituisci uno dei cassetti stretti con un vassoio estraibile, che potrai utilizzare come piano aggiuntivo.

Substitua uma das gavetas mais estreitas por uma prateleira extraível que funciona como mesa auxiliar.

Ersätt en av de smala lådorna med en utdragbar skiva som fungerar som avlastningsbord.

Instead of several small closets it is better to have a spacious bar and storage units under the sink. This will keep the upper half of the kitchen clutter-free.

Au lieu de plusieurs petits placards, il vaut mieux disposer d'un plan très large et de meubles de rangement sous l'évier. De cette façon, on allège la partie supérieure de la cuisine.

Statt mehrerer kleiner Schränke ist es besser, über eine breite Theke und Schränke unter der Spüle zu verfügen. Auf diese Weise bleibt die obere Hälfte der Küche frei.

In plaats van verschillende kleinere kasten is het beter om te beschikken over een ruime bar en lage meubels onder de gootsteen voor opbergruimte. Op die manier blijft de bovenste helft van de keuken vrij.

En lugar de varios armarios pequeños es mejor disponer una amplia barra y muebles bajo el fregadero para el almacenaje. De este modo se mantiene despejada la mitad superior de la cocina.

Al posto di tanti mobili stretti, è meglio disporre di un ampio bancone e mobili di contenimento sotto il lavello. In tal modo sarà libera la metà superiore della cucina.

Em lugar de vários armários pequenos é melhor dispor de um balcão amplo e móveis sob o lava-louça para arrumação. Deste modo a metade superior da cozinha mantém-se desocupada.

Istället för flera små skåp är det bättre med en bred arbetsyta och förvaringsskåp under diskbänken. På så sätt hålls den övre halvan av köket fritt.

Add a touch of style to the kitchen with high designer stools at the bar.

Ces tabourets de bar design apportent une touche de style à la cuisine.

Verleihen Sie der Küche mit hohen Designer-Hockern vor der Theke eine stilvolle Atmosphäre.

Geef de keuken iets stijlvols met hoge design krukken aan de bar.

Aplica un toque de estilo a la cocina con unos taburetes altos de diseño frente a la barra.

Applica un tocco di stile alla cucina con sgabelli alti di design posti davanti al bancone.

Aplique um toque de estilo à cozinha colocando uns bancos altos de design em frente ao balcão.

Ge köket distinktion med höga designbarstolar framför bardisken.

Install an elongated island in the American kitchen. It is a great way to separate the living room from this space with a fully functional object.

Installer un îlot allongé devant la cuisine américaine est une excellente manière de séparer cet espace du salon grâce à un meuble complètement fonctionnel.

Bauen Sie eine verlängerte Insel vor die Amerikanische Küche. Das ist eine ausgezeichnete Art, diesen Bereich vom Wohnzimmer mit einem vollkommen funktionalen Möbelstück zu trennen.

Installeer een langwerpig eiland tegenover een open keuken. Dat is een uitstekende manier om deze ruimte af te scheiden van de zitkamer met een uiterst functioneel ontwerp.

Instala una isla alargada frente a la cocina americana. Es una excelente manera de separar este ambiente del salón con un objeto totalmente funcional.

Installa un'isola allungata davanti alla cucina all'americana. È una soluzione che ti consentirà di separare questo ambiente dalla sala con un oggetto totalmente funzionale.

Instale uma ilha alongada em frente à cozinha americana. É uma excelente maneira de separar este espaço da sala com um objecto totalmente funcional.

Placera en avlång köksö framför köksmöblerna. Det är ett utmärkt sätt att skilja köket från vardagsrummet med ett mycket funktionellt objekt.

Define the breakfast table with lighting and decoration that are different from the rest of the kitchen.

Vous pouvez délimiter la zone repas du reste de la cuisine par un éclairage et une décoration indépendants.

Grenzen Sie den Bereich des *office* (des Essplatzes) mit einer von der übrigen Küche unabhängigen Beleuchtung und Dekoration ab.

Baken de zone van de *office* af met verlichting en decoratie die onafhankelijk is van de rest van de woning.

Define la zona del *office* con una iluminación y una decoración independientes del resto de la cocina.

Definisci la zona *office* con un'illuminazione e arredi indipendenti dal resto della cucina.

Defina a zona do *office* com uma iluminação e uma decoração independentes do resto da cozinha.

Definiera matvrån med belysning och inredning som skiljer sig från resten av köket.

The dining room should be designed with the same materials that prevail in this space so that it naturally integrates.

Il est préférable que la table à manger et les chaises de la cuisine soient réalisées dans les mêmes matériaux que les autres éléments de cet espace pour qu'ils s'y intègrent naturellement.

Der Essbereich sollte vorzugsweise aus denselben Materialien bestehen, die in der Küche vorherrschen, damit er sich natürlich einfügt.

De eethoek in de keuken moet bij voorkeur worden samengesteld uit de materialen die ook overheersen in deze ruimte voor een natuurlijke integratie.

Es preferible que el comedor de la cocina esté compuesto de los mismos materiales que imperan en este ambiente para que quede naturalmente integrado.

È preferibile che il tinello della cucina sia composto dagli stessi materiali che predominano in questo ambiente affinché vi sia una naturale uniformità.

É preferível que a área de refeições da cozinha seja composta pelos mesmos materiais que prevalecem neste espaço para que se integre naturalmente.

Det är att föredra att matplatsen i köket består av samma material som råder i resten av detta rum, så att den integreras.

Situate the dining room between the open kitchen and living room and you can intimately integrate these spaces that are used so often on a daily basis.

Installer la salle à manger entre la cuisine ouverte et le salon permet de réunir ces espaces de la vie quotidienne si intimement reliés.

Installieren Sie den Essbereich zwischen Küche und Wohnzimmer, so können Sie diese Räume, die für das tägliche Leben so wichtig sind, verbinden.

Plaats de eetkamer tussen de open keuken en de zitkamer in. Zo kunt u deze ruimtes die zo zijn verbonden met het dagelijkse leven integreren.

Instala el comedor entre la cocina abierta y el salón y podrás integrar estos ambientes tan íntimamente relacionados de la vida cotidiana.

Sistema il tinello tra la cucina aperta e il salotto e potrai così integrare questi due ambienti così intimamente collegati della vita quotidiana

Instale a sala de jantar entre a cozinha aberta e a sala e assim será possível integrar estes ambientes tão intimamente relacionados com a vida quotidiana.

Placera matsalen mellan det öppna köket och vardagsrummet. På så sätt kan du förena dessa två utrymmen som används så mycket dagligen.

Place the dinner table right next to the island and you will have an additional surface to place dishes, trays, bottles and bread baskets while eating.

Coller la table à manger à l'îlot de la cuisine augmente la surface servant de support aux plats, plateaux, bouteilles et corbeilles à pain pendant les repas.

Platzieren Sie den Esstisch dicht an die Insel und gewinnen Sie so einen zusätzliche Fläche zum Abstellen von Schüsseln, Flaschen und Brotkörben während des Essens.

Zet de eettafel tegen het eiland aan. Zo verkrijgt u extra ruimte om schalen, bladen, flessen en broodmanden op te zetten tijdens de maaltijd.

Sitúa la mesa del comedor pegada a la isla y gana una superficie auxiliar para apoyar fuentes, bandejas, botellas y paneras mientras se come.

Posiziona il tavolo del tinello accanto all'isola per guadagnare una superficie aggiuntiva su cui appoggiare piatti, vassoi, bottiglie e portapane durante i pasti.

Coloque a mesa de refeições junto à ilha e ganhe uma superfície auxiliar para apoiar recipientes, tabuleiros, garrafas e cestas do pão enquanto come.

Placera matsalsbordet bredvid köksön så har du ett extra avlastningsbord för brickor, uppläggningsfat, flaskor och brödkorgar under måltiden.

The kitchen dining room should have enough room to move comfortably, with a suitable size table and chairs that fit in easily.

La table à manger et les chaises de la cuisine doivent bien évidemment aller ensemble et laisser la place suffisante pour bouger aisément.

Der Essbereich der Küche sollte mit einem Tisch von entsprechender Größe und Stühlen, die sich leicht stapeln lassen, genügend Bewegungsfreiheit bieten.

De eethoek van de keuken moet voldoende ruimte overlaten zodat men zich comfortabel kan bewegen, met een tafel van geschikte afmetingen en stoelen die eenvoudig kunnen worden aangeschoven.

El comedor de la cocina debe dejar suficiente espacio para moverse con comodidad, con una mesa de dimensiones adecuadas y sillas que se acoplen fácilmente.

Il tinello della cucina deve lasciare spazio sufficiente per muoversi comodamente, con un tavolo di dimensioni adeguate e sedie facilmente accostabili.

A área de refeições da cozinha deve deixar espaço suficiente para que se possa mover comodamente, com uma mesa de dimensões adequadas e cadeiras que se ajustem facilmente.

Kökets matvrå bör ha tillräckligt med plats för att man lätt ska kunna röra sig, men ett bord av lämplig storlek och stolar som passar det.

Install good lighting in particular above the worktop. Besides being very useful when handling food, light adds warmth to the kitchen, as opposed to cold lighting on the ceiling.

Un bon éclairage du plan de travail aide à mieux manipuler les aliments et réchauffe l'atmosphère de la cuisine, contrairement à l'éclairage froid du plafond.

Beleuchten Sie besonders die Arbeitsfläche. Außer, dass diese Beleuchtung bei der Handhabung der Lebensmittel sehr nützlich ist, bringt sie im Gegensatz zu der kalten Deckenbeleuchtung Wärme in die Küche.

Zorg vooral voor een goede verlichting van het aanrecht. Behalve dat dat nuttig is bij het bereiden van het eten, geeft het licht warmte in de keuken, tegenover de koele plafondverlichting.

Ilumina especialmente la encimera. Además de ser muy útil a la hora de manipular los alimentos, la luz otorga calidez a la cocina, en contraposición a la iluminación fría del techo.

Illumina soprattutto il ripiano della cucina. Oltre a essere molto utile quando si preparano i cibi, la luce trasmette calore alla cucina, in contrasto con l'illuminazione fredda dei lampadari a soffitto.

Ilumine especialmente a bancada. Além de se tornar muito útil na altura de manipular os alimentos, a luz transmite calor à cozinha, contrariamente à iluminação fria do tecto.

Det är speciellt viktigt att belysa arbetsytan. Förutom att det är praktiskt vid matlagning, ger ljuset värme åt köket, i motsats till det kalla takljuset.

A rustic kitchen can become a very welcoming and practical space by combining wood and steel, simple, solid pieces of furniture and natural fiber stools.

L'association du bois et de l'acier, de meubles simples et solides et de tabourets en fibre naturelle donne à la cuisine rustique un aspect accueillant et pratique.

Eine rustikale Küche kann durch die Kombination von Holz und Stahl, einfachen und stabilen Möbeln und Hockern aus Naturfasern sowohl gemütlich als auch praktisch sein.

Een landelijke keuken kan worden omgebouwd tot een gezellige en praktische ruimte met de combinatie hout en staal, eenvoudige en solide meubels en krukken van natuurvezel.

La cocina rústica se puede convertir en un ambiente tan acogedor como práctico con la combinación de madera y acero, muebles sencillos y sólidos y taburetes de fibra natural.

La cucina rustica può trasformarsi in un ambiente pratico e accogliente, combinando legno e acciaio, mobili semplici e solidi con sgabelli in fibra naturale.

A cozinha rústica pode tornar-se um ambiente tão acolhedor como prático através da combinação de madeira e aço, móveis simples e robustos, e bancos de fibra natural.

Ett lantligt kök kan förvandlas till en hemtrevlig och praktisk miljö med en kombination av trä och stål, enkla och stabila möbler och pallar av naturmaterial.

Opt for skylights in the ceiling or upper part of the wall to flood the kitchen with natural light.

Des ouvertures au plafond ou dans la partie supérieure des murs inondent la cuisine de lumière naturelle.

Verwenden Sie Oberlichter in der Decke oder im oberen Teil der Wände, um natürliches Licht in die Küche zu lassen.

Neem uw toevlucht tot dakramen in het plafond of bovenaan de muren om uw keuken in het daglicht te zetten.

Recurre a los tragaluces en el techo o la parte superior de las paredes para inundar de luz natural la cocina.

Sfrutta i lucernari a soffitto o la parte superiore delle pareti per inondare di luce naturale la cucina.

Recorra a clarabóias no tecto ou na parte superior das paredes para inundar a cozinha com luz natural.

Använd skylights i taket eller den övre delen av väggarna för att ge köket mycket naturligt ljus.

Do not neglect the decor of the dining area just because it is incorporated into the kitchen. Rugs can also be used in this space. Just leave a free strip on the floor in front of the worktop.

La décoration de la salle à manger ne doit pas être négligée sous prétexte qu'elle se trouve dans l'espace de la cuisine. Les tapis ont aussi leur importance. Il faut juste laisser un couloir libre devant le plan de travail.

Vernachlässigen Sie die Dekoration des Essbereiches nicht, weil er in die Küche integriert ist. Teppiche sind auch für diesen Raum geeignet. Lassen Sie nur einen freien Gang auf dem Boden vor der Arbeitsfläche.

Veronachtzaam de decoratie van de eetkamer niet omdat deze in de keuken ligt. Ook vloerkleden zijn geschikt voor deze ruimte. Laat alleen een strook open op de grond voor het aanrecht.

No descuides la decoración de la zona del comedor por estar incluida en la cocina. Las alfombras también valen en este espacio. Solo deja un pasillo libre en el suelo frente a la encimera.

Non tralasciare gli arredi della zona del tinello, che sarà così integrata nella cucina. In questo spazio possono essere utilizzati anche dei tappeti. Lascia solo un corridoio libero davanti al piano della cucina.

Não descuide a decoração da área de refeições por fazer parte da cozinha. Os tapetes também têm um papel importante neste espaço. Deixe apenas um corredor livre no solo em frente à bancada.

Försumma inte inredningen av matvrån bara för att det är en del av köket. Här kan man också använda mattor. Lämna bara golvet framför arbetsytan tom.

Use lamps to emphasize the definition of the breakfast table in the kitchen and provide good lighting to the area where you eat.

Vous pouvez utiliser les lampes pour mieux délimiter l'espace de la zone repas dans la cuisine et l'éclairer convenablement.

Verwenden Sie die Lampen, um den Bereich des *office* in der Küche abzugrenzen und den Essplatz gut zu beleuchten.

Maak gebruik van lampen om de afbakening van de *office* in de keuken te versterken en zorg voor een goede verlichting van de eethoek.

Usa las lámparas para reforzar la definición del espacio del *office* en la cocina e iluminar muy bien la zona donde se come.

Usa i punti luce per rafforzare la definizione dello spazio *office* in cucina e illuminare molto bene la zona in cui si mangia.

Use os candeeiros para reforçar a definição do espaço do *office* na cozinha e iluminar muito bem a zona das refeições.

Använd lampor för att förstärka kökets matvrå och belysa matplatsen ordentligt.

Black has taken over the modern and stylish kitchens. But the area where food is handled and cooked should be in a contrasting color, preferably white.

Le noir a pris possession des cuisines modernes et élégantes. Toutefois, les plans de travail et de cuisson doivent avoir une couleur qui se détache de l'ensemble, de préférence le blanc.

Schwarz hat sich der modernen, eleganten Küchen bemächtigt. Aber die Bereiche für die Verarbeitung und das Kochen von Lebensmitteln sollten in einer kontrastierenden Farbe, vorzugsweise weiß, gehalten sein.

Zwart is toonaangevend in moderne en elegante keukens. Maar de plaats waar men het eten bereikt en kookt moet een contrasterende kleur hebben, bij voorkeur wit.

El negro se ha apoderado de las cocinas modernas y elegantes. Pero la zona de manipulación y cocción de los alimentos debe permanecer en un color que contraste, preferentemente blanco.

Il nero ha conquistato le cucine moderne ed eleganti. La zona di lavoro e cottura deve però essere in un colore contrastante, preferibilmente bianco.

A cor preta apoderou-se das cozinhas modernas e elegantes. Mas a zona de manipulação e confecção dos alimentos deve permanecer numa cor que contraste, de preferência a cor branca.

Svart har blivit populärt i moderna och eleganta kök. Men platser där man tillreder och lagar maten bör vara i en kontrasterande färg, helst vit.

Modern appliances have abandoned the traditional white and steel colors to incorporate beautiful colors that add a special touch to the kitchen.

Les appareils électroménagers modernes ont quitté la dictature du blanc et de l'acier pour revêtir des couleurs vives apportant une touche spéciale à la cuisine.

Die modernen elektrischen Haushaltsgeräte unterwerfen sich nicht mehr der Diktatur von Weiß und Stahl. Es gibt sie heute in attraktiven Farben, die der Küche eine besondere Note verleihen.

De moderne huishoudelijke apparaten zijn allang niet meer alleen wit en van staal, maar hebben tegenwoordig aantrekkelijke kleuren die de keuken een speciaal accent geven.

Los electrodomésticos modernos han abandonado la dictadura del blanco y el acero para incorporar atractivos colores que dan un toque especial a la cocina.

Gli elettrodomestici moderni hanno abbandonato la "dittatura" del bianco e dell'acciaio per integrare colori vivaci che conferiscono un tocco speciale alla cucina.

Os electrodomésticos modernos abandonaram a ditadura da cor branca e do aço para incorporar cores atractivas que dão um toque especial à cozinha.

Moderna vitvaror finns inte bara i vitt och stål utan även i attraktiva färger som ger en speciell känsla åt köket.

Some worktop models are specially designed as troughs that bring water directly to the sink and therefore pools of water do not form, or metal strips that serve as a trivet.

Certains modèles de plan de travail ont un design particulier, comme les petites canalisations conduisant l'eau directement à l'évier et faisant disparaître les résidus liquides ou les barres métalliques servant de dessous-de-plat.

Manche Arbeitsplattenmodelle haben ein besonderes Design, wie z.B. Metall-Leisten in der Art von Untersetzern oder Abflussrinnen, die das Wasser direkt in das Spülbecken leiten und die Pfützen verschwinden lassen.

Sommige modellen werkbladen hebben een speciaal ontwerp, zoals gootjes die het water rechtstreeks naar de gootsteen leiden, zodat er geen plasjes ontstaan, of metalen stroken die dienst doen als placemats.

Algunos modelos de encimeras tienen un diseño especial, como las canaletas que conducen el agua directamente al fregadero y hacen desaparecer los charcos, o las barras metálicas a modo de salvamanteles.

Alcuni modelli di ripiani hanno un design speciale come dei canalini di scolo che fanno scorrere l'acqua direttamente nel lavello eliminando le pozze o barrette metalliche per far asciugare gli oggetti bagnati.

Alguns modelos de bancadas têm um design especial como os canais que conduzem a água directamente para o lava-louça e fazem desaparecer a água acumulada, ou as barras metálicas para apoio de utensílios.

Vissa arbetsytor har en speciell utformning, som t.ex. rännor som leder vattnet direkt ned i diskhon och gör att man slipper pölar, eller metallstänger som fungerar som grytunderlägg.

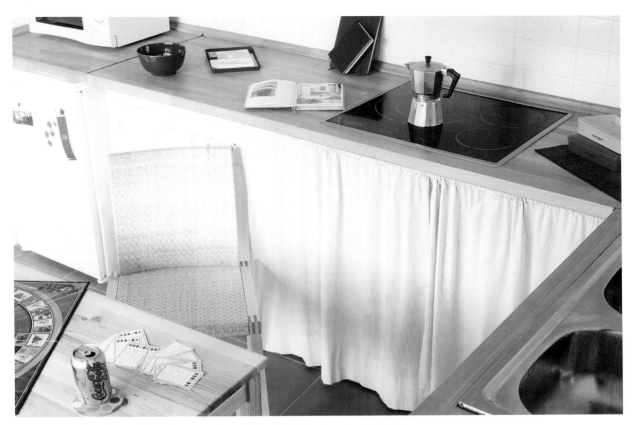

The curtains below the worktop are still a good resource to keep shelves and their contents out of sight. Opt for white or a solid color, without prints, to give the kitchen a modern look.

Les rideaux en bas de l'évier sont toujours un bon moyen pour cacher les étagères et leur contenu. Idéalement, elles sont blanches ou d'une couleur unie, sans dessins imprimés, ce qui leur confère un air moderne.

Vorhänge unter der Arbeitsfläche sind immer noch ein gutes Mittel, Regale und deren Inhalt zu verbergen. Umso besser, wenn sie weiß oder einfarbig, und ungemustert sind, damit sie modern wirken.

Gordijnen onder het aanrecht zijn nog steeds een handig hulpmiddel om planken en de inhoud daarvan te verbergen. Wit of een effen kleur, zonder opdruk, zijn de beste keuze, voor een moderne aanblik.

Las cortinillas debajo de la encimera siguen siendo un buen un recurso para mantener fuera de la vista los estantes y sus contenidos. Mejor si es blanca o de un color liso, sin estampados, para darle un aire moderno.

Le tendine sotto il piano di lavoro continuano a essere una buona soluzione per nascondere i ripiani e il loro contenuto. Meglio optare per il bianco o un colore unico, senza stampe, per renderle più moderne.

As cortinas debaixo da bancada continuam a ser um bom recurso para manter fora da vista as estantes e os seus conteúdos. É recomendável que seja branca ou de uma cor lisa, sem estampados, para que tenha um ar moderno.

Ett skynke under arbetsytan är fortfarande en bra lösning för att dölja hyllorna och dess innehåll. Det bör helst vara vitt eller enfärgat, inte mönstrat, för ett ge ett modernt intryck.

Ceramic materials for flooring, including different types of sandstone and clay, are all very durable, easy to clean and available in a wide range of finishes and colors.

Les carrelages pour le sol – des différents types de grès à la terre cuite – sont tous très résistants, faciles à nettoyer et ils présentent une large gamme de finitions et de couleurs.

Die verschiedenen Keramikmaterialien für den Boden von Steingut bis gebranntem Ton sind alle sehr hart, leicht zu reinigen und in vielen unterschiedlichen Ausführungen und Farben erhältlich.

Keramiek materialen voor de vloer, vanaf verschillende soorten aardewerk tot gebakken klei, zijn alle zeer hard, eenvoudig schoon te maken en met een waaier aan afwerkingen en kleuren.

Los materiales cerámicos para el suelo, desde diferentes tipos de gres hasta barro cocido, son todos de gran dureza, fáciles de limpiar y con una amplia gama de acabados y colores.

I materiali ceramici per pavimenti, dai vari tipi di gres al cotto, sono tutti molto resistenti, facili da pulire e disponibili in un'ampia gamma di finiture e colori.

Os materiais cerâmicos para o solo, desde diferentes tipos de grês a terracota, são todos muito resistentes, fáceis de limpar e com uma ampla gama de acabamentos e cores.

Keramikmaterial för golvet, från olika typer av stengods till bränd lera, är alla mycket hårda material som är enkla att rengöra och finns i ett stort utbud av utföranden och färger.

Although, in theory, wood is not the best choice for kitchen flooring, thanks to modern pore sealing treatments, extremely hard-wearing floors are available that give warmth to this space.

Même si, à l'origine, le bois n'est pas le revêtement le plus adapté au sol de la cuisine, il apporte de la chaleur à cette pièce. Ils en existent actuellement de très résistants, grâce à des traitements modernes qui augmentent leur étanchéité.

Auch wenn Holz grundsätzlich nicht der beste Bodenbelag für eine Küche ist, gibt es dank der modernen Versiegelungstechniken sehr widerstandsfähige Böden, die diesem Raum Wärme verleihen.

Hoewel een houten vloer in principe niet geschikt is voor de keuken, bestaan er dankzij de moderne behandelingen waarmee de poriën worden afgedicht zeer bestendige vloeren die deze ruimte de nodige warmte geven.

Aunque, en principio, la madera no es el mejor pavimento para una cocina, gracias a los modernos tratamientos de sellado de poro existen suelos muy resistentes que le dan calidez a este espacio.

Anche se in teoria il legno non è il pavimento migliore per una cucina, grazie ai moderni trattamenti di sigillatura dei pori, sono disponibili soluzioni molto resistenti che trasmettono grande calore a questo spazio.

Embora em princípio a madeira não seja o melhor pavimento para uma cozinha, graças aos modernos tratamentos de selagem de poros, existem solos muito resistentes que conferem calor a este espaço.

Även om trä inte är det bästa golvvalet för ett kök, finns det tack vare moderna förseglingstekniker mycket resistenta trägolv som ger värme åt detta rum.

In small kitchens, use sliding doors or walls and glass partitions to save space and allow sufficient light through.

Si la cuisine est petite, les portes coulissantes ou les cloisons en verre permettent d'optimiser l'espace et de laisser entrer la lumière.

In kleinen Küchen installieren Sie Schiebetüren oder Zwischenwände mit Glas, um Platz zu sparen und Licht einzulassen.

Neem in kleine keukens uw toevlucht tot schuifpuien of glazen tussenmuurtjes om ruimte te besparen en licht te laten invallen.

En cocinas pequeñas, recurre a cerramientos como puertas correderas o tabiques con cristal para ahorrar espacio y dejar entrar la luz.

Nelle cucine piccole opta per porte scorrevoli o divisori in vetro per risparmiare spazio e lasciar passare la luce.

Em cozinhas pequenas, recorra a soluções como portas de correr ou divisórias com vidro para poupar espaço e deixar entrar a luz.

I små kök kan man använda skjutdörrar eller mellanväggar av glas för att spara plats och släppa in ljus.

Create a vibrant, stunning kitchen with vinyl on the wall with the image of a market stall. The resistance of this material to steam and heat guarantees it to be long-lasting.

Ce vinyle décoratif mural représentant un étalage du marché crée un effet de surprise très réussi dans cette cuisine. La résistance de ces stickers à la vapeur et à la chaleur leur assure une longue durée de vie.

Schaffen Sie eine überraschende und beschwingte Küche mit einer Vinyltapete, die einen Marktstand vortäuscht. Die Resistenz dieses Materials gegen Dämpfe und Hitze garantiert eine lange Lebensdauer.

Creëer een verrassende en levendige keuken met vinyl op de muren waarop een marktkraam is afgebeeld. De bestendigheid van dit materiaal tegen stoom en warmte garandeert een lange levensduur.

Crea una cocina sorprendente y vibrante con un vinilo en la pared que simula el puesto de un mercado. La resistencia de este material a los vapores y el calor asegura una larga permanencia.

Crea una cucina sorprendente e vivace con una stampa in vinile che riproduce un banco del mercato. La resistenza di questo materiale ai vapori e al calore ne garantisce una lunga durata.

Crie uma cozinha surpreendente e vibrante aplicando na parede um vinil que simula a banca de um mercado. A resistência deste material aos vapores e ao calor assegura uma longa permanência.

Skapa ett överraskande och livfullt kök med en vinylbild i köket som avbildar ett marknadsstånd. Detta material är mycket hållbart mot ånga och värme och håller länge.

Separate the kitchen from the dining room with a glass expanse with motifs associated with the kitchen such as recipes or images of accessories.

La cuisine peut être séparée de la salle à manger par une cloison en verre ornée de motifs liés à la cuisine, tels des recettes ou des dessins d'accessoires.

Trennen Sie die Küche vom Essplatz mit einer Glasscheibe, die mit Küchenmotiven wie Rezepten oder Zeichnungen von Küchengeräten dekoriert ist, ab.

Scheid de keuken van de eetkamer af door glas met motieven die te maken hebben met de keuken, zoals recepten of tekeningen van accessoires.

Separa la cocina del comedor con un cristal con motivos vinculados a la cocina como recetas o dibujos de accesorios.

Separa la cucina dal tinello con un vetro arricchito da motivi legati alla cucina come ricette o disegni di accessori.

Separe a cozinha da sala de jantar utilizando um vidro decorado com motivos de referência à cozinha tais como receitas ou desenhos de acessórios.

Skilj köket från matsalen med en glasvägg med köksmotiv, som recept eller bilder på köksredskap.

Even if the kitchen is very small, there's always room for a decorative detail that makes it a pleasant space. Use drawings on the wall or an original, eye-catching clock.

Même si la cuisine est très petite, il y a toujours de la place pour un détail décoratif : des dessins sur le mur ou une pendule originale constituent des solutions intéressantes.

Auch wenn die Küche sehr klein ist, gibt es immer Platz für ein dekoratives Detail, das sie in einen gemütlichen Raum verwandelt. Dekorieren Sie die Wand mit graphischen Motiven oder einer originellen, auffallenden Uhr.

Ook al is de keuken klein, er is altijd wel een plekje voor een decoratief detail om er een aangename ruimte van te maken. Denk aan muurtekeningen of een originele, opvallende klok.

Aunque la cocina sea muy pequeñita, siempre hay espacio para un detalle decorativo que la convierta en un espacio agradable. Recurre a dibujos en la pared o un reloj original y llamativo.

Anche se la cucina è molto piccola, c'è sempre spazio per un dettaglio decorativo che la trasformi in uno ambiente piacevole. Opta per disegni da applicare sulla parete o per un orologio appariscente e originale.

Ainda que a cozinha possa ser muito pequena, há sempre espaço para um pormenor decorativo que a converta num espaço agradável. Recorra a desenhos na parede ou a um relógio original e chamativo.

Även om köket är litet finns det alltid plats för ett dekorativt föremål som förvandlar det till en behaglig plats. Du kan hänga teckningar på väggen eller kanske en originell och uppseendeväckande klocka.

CHILDREN'S BEDROOM
CHAMBRE D'ENFANT
KINDERZIMMER
KINDERKAMER
DORMITORIO INFANTIL
CAMERA DEI BAMBINI
QUARTO DAS CRIANÇAS
BARNRUMMET

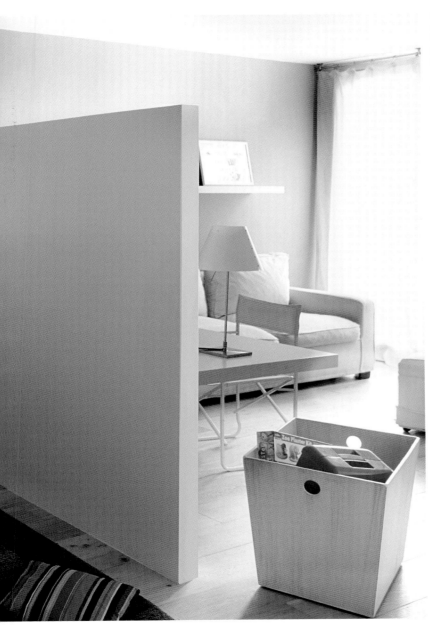

Place a partition in the middle of the room that serves as a support for one of the beds and separates the rest area from the play area.

La cloison au centre de la pièce sert de support à l'un des lits et sépare le coin repos du coin jeu.

Bringen Sie in der Zimmermitte eine Trennwand an, die als Stützwand für eins der Betten dient und den Schlaf- vom Spielbereich trennt.

Plaats een tussenmuur midden in de kamer als steun voor een van de bedden en scheid het slaapgedeelte af van het speelgedeelte.

Coloca un tabique en el medio de la habitación que sirva como soporte a una de las camas y separe la zona de descanso de la de juego.

Sistema un divisorio al centro della stanza, servirà da supporto a uno dei letti e separerà la zona notte da quella dedicata al gioco.

Coloque uma divisória no meio do quarto que sirva de suporte a uma das camas e que separe a zona de descanso da zona de brincar.

Placera en vägg i mitten av rummet som stöd för en av sängarna och som skiljer viloutrymmet från lekutrymmet.

A bunk bed with a zigzag structure provides storage capacity, as the high bed rests on a closet.

Les lits superposés décalés augmentent la capacité de rangement, car le lit en haut repose sur une armoire.

Mit einem zickzackförmig angebrachten Etagenbett gewinnt man Stauraum, da das Hochbett auf einem Schrank aufliegt.

Met een zig-zag stapelbed heeft u meer opbergruimte, aangezien het bovenste bed op een kledingkast steunt.

Con una litera en zigzag se gana capacidad de almacenaje, ya que la cama alta se apoya sobre un armario.

Con un letto a castello sfalsato si guadagna contenimento poiché il letto superiore poggia su un armadio.

Recorrendo a um beliche em ziguezague é possível ganhar capacidade de arrumação visto que a cama superior é apoiada sobre um armário.

Med en våningssäng i vinkel får man ökat förvaringsutrymme eftersom den högre sängen vilar på en garderob.

Take advantage of an almost square room with two beds at an angle or facing each other and another higher bed accessed via a ladder.

On peut tirer parti d'une chambre presque carrée avec deux lits d'angle ou côte à côte et un autre placé au-dessus, auquel on accède par une échelle.

Nutzen Sie ein Zimmer mit fast quadratischem Grundriss aus, und stellen Sie zwei Betten rechtwinklig zueinander oder gegenüber auf und installieren Sie ein weiteres, das man mit einer Leiter erreicht, sehr hoch darüber.

Benut een slaapmaker met vierkant grondplan optimaal met twee bedden in een hoek of tegenover elkaar en een bed daarboven, met een trap.

Saca partido a un dormitorio de planta casi cuadrada con dos camas en ángulo o enfrentadas y otra elevada muy por encima a la que se accede mediante una escalera.

Sfrutta al massimo una camera a pianta quasi quadrata con due letti ad angolo o posti uno davanti all'altro e un altro molto elevato, accessibile tramite una scala.

Tire partido de um quarto de planta quase quadrada colocando duas camas em ângulo ou face a face e outra elevada muito por cima à qual se pode aceder por meio de uma escada.

Dra fordel av et nesten kvadratisk soverom med to senger i vinkel og en annen hevet høyt over de andre som en bruker stige for å komme opp til.

Use the space under the bed to store boxes and drawers with clothes and toys.

L'espace sous le lit peut accueillir des boîtes et des tiroirs pour ranger des vêtements et des jouets.

Nutzen Sie den Platz unter dem Bett aus, um Kästen und Schubladen mit Wäsche oder Spielzeug unterzubringen.

Benut de ruimte onder het bed voor laden om kleding of speelgoed in te bewaren.

Aprovecha el espacio debajo de la cama para poner cajas y cajones con ropa o juguetes.

Sfrutta lo spazio sotto il letto per sistemare scatole e cassetti contenenti vestiti o giochi.

Aproveite o espaço debaixo da cama para colocar caixas e gavetas com roupa ou brinquedos.

Utnyttja utrymmet under sängen för att placera lådor med kläder eller leksaker där.

Personalize the children's bedroom with decorative objects that also help maintain order, such as this coat rack reminiscent of a school rack.

La chambre d'enfant peut être personnalisée avec des objets de décoration qui servent aussi de rangement, comme ce porte-manteau rappelant l'école.

Geben Sie dem Kinderzimmer eine persönliche Note mit dekorativen Objekten, die zudem helfen, Ordnung zu halten, wie dieser Kleiderständer, der an diejenigen erinnert, die es in der Schule gibt.

Maak de kinderkamer persoonlijk met decoratieve voorwerpen zodat die er bovendien opgeruimder uitziet, zoals deze kapstok die doet denken aan die van school.

Personaliza el dormitorio infantil con objetos decorativos que además ayuden a mantener el orden, como este perchero que recuerda a los del colegio.

Personalizza la camera da letto dei bambini con oggetti che contribuiscano anche a mantenere l'ordine, come questo appendiabiti che ricorda quelli di scuola.

Personalize o quarto das crianças com objectos decorativos que ajudem também a manter a ordem, como este cabide que evoca os da escola.

Gör sovrummet mer personligt med dekorativa föremål som även hjälper till att hålla ordning, som denna klädhängare som ser ut att komma från en skola.

So that the wallpaper print is not too overwhelming, cover three quarters of the area and leave the top part white.

Pour ne pas se lasser du papier peint, il suffit de ne couvrir que trois quarts de la surface et de laisser la partie supérieure en blanc.

Damit das Tapetenmuster nicht erdrückend wirkt, tapezieren Sie drei Viertel der Fläche und lassen Sie den oberen Teil weiß.

Behang hoeft niet meer overladen te zijn als u drie vierde van het oppervlak behangt en de bovenkant wit laat.

Para que el estampado del papel de pared no resulte agobiante, cubre tres cuartos de la superficie y deja la parte superior en blanco.

Affinche la stampa della carta da parati non risulti eccessivamente pesante, copri tre quarti della superficie e lascia bianca la parte superiore.

Para que o estampado do papel de parede não se torne excessivo, cubra três quartos da superfície e deixe a parte superior a branco.

För att tapetmönstret inte ska bli överväldigande kan man bara täcka tre fjärdedelar av ytan och låta resten vara vit.

If there is space in the master bedroom for the baby's crib, use a chest of drawers at the foot of the large bed to separate the spaces.

Si dans la chambre à coucher principale il y a de la place pour le berceau du bébé, on peut séparer les espaces avec une commode à roulette installée au pied du grand lit.

Wenn es im Elternschlafzimmer Platz für eine Wiege gibt, stellen Sie eine Kommode am Fußende des Doppelbetts auf, um den Raum zu unterteilen.

Is er voldoende ruimte in de slaapkamer voor een wieg, gebruik dan een commode aan de voet van het grote bed om de ruimtes te scheiden.

Si hay espacio en el dormitorio principal para la cuna del bebé, utiliza una cómoda a los pies de la cama grande para separar los ambientes.

Se nella camera dei genitori c'è spazio per la culla, utilizza un comò ai piedi del letto matrimoniale per separare i due ambienti.

Caso exista espaço no quarto principal para o berço do bebé, utilize uma cómoda aos pés da cama para separar os espaços.

Om det finns plats för vaggan i föräldrarnas sovrum kan man använda en byrå vid sängens fotända för att skilja av rummet.

Maintain visual continuity using colors from the same family (such as cool colors, blue, green, violet or cyan). This creates an environment that conveys serenity, suitable for children's rooms.

Maintenir la continuité visuelle en utilisant des couleurs de la même famille – comme des couleurs froides, le bleu, le vert, le violet ou le cyan – crée une atmosphère sereine très adaptée aux chambres d'enfant.

Erhalten Sie das einheitliche Aussehen durch Farben derselben Familie (wie kalte Farben, Blau, Grün, Violett oder Türkis). Auf diese Weise wird eine ruhige Atmosphäre geschaffen, die für Kinderzimmer sehr geeignet ist.

Behoud de visuele continuïteit door gebruik te maken van kleuren van dezelfde familie (zoals koude kleuren, blauw, groen, violet of cyaan). Op die manier creëert u een ruimte die rust uitstraalt, zeer geschikt voor kinderkamers.

Mantén la continuidad visual usando colores de la misma familia (como colores fríos, azul, verde, violeta o cian). Así se crea un ambiente que transmite serenidad, muy adecuado en cuartos infantiles.

Mantieni la continuità visiva utilizzando colori della stessa famiglia (ad esempio colori freddi: blu, verde, viola o ciano). In tal modo creerai un ambiente che trasmette serenità, particolarmente adatto ai più piccoli.

Mantenha a continuidade visual usando cores da mesma família (como cores frias, azul, verde, roxo ou ciano). Deste modo é criado um espaço que transmite serenidade, muito adequado em quartos infantis.

Behåll den visuella kontinuiteten genom att använda färger i samma skala (som t.ex. kalla färger som blått, grönt, lila och turkost.) Så skapar man en miljö som inger lugn och som är mycket lämplig i barnrum.

Even though the bedroom is large, leave as much space as possible to let children play, jump and run. Do not cram it with furniture.

Même si la chambre est grande, il faut laisser le plus d'espace possible pour que les enfants jouent, sautent et courent, sans la remplir de meubles.

Auch wenn das Zimmer groß ist, lassen Sie so viel Platz wie möglich frei, damit die Kinder spielen, springen und rennen können. Überladen Sie es nicht mit Möbeln.

Laat, ook bij grote slaapkamers, zo veel mogelijk ruimte leeg zodat kinderen er kunnen spelen, springen en rennen. Zet de slaapkamer niet vol met meubels.

Aunque el dormitorio sea grande, deja la mayor cantidad de espacio que se pueda para que los niños jueguen, salten y corran. No lo llenes de muebles.

Anche se la camera è grande, lascia libero quanto più spazio possibile affinché i bambini possano giocare, saltare e correre. Non riempire gli ambienti di mobili.

Embora o quarto seja grande, deixe disponível a maior quantidade de espaço possível para que as crianças possam brincar, saltar e correr. Não encha o quarto com demasiados móveis.

Även om rummet är stort bör man lämna så stort utrymme som möjligt fritt så att barnen kan leka, hoppa och springa. Ha inte för mycket möbler.

Boxes or baskets are very practical for storing toys in a quick and easy manner, and to get kids used to tidying up when they finish playing.

Les boîtes ou les paniers sont très pratiques pour ranger de manière facile et rapide les jouets et habituer les enfants à remettre les affaires à leur place quand ils ont terminé de jouer.

Kästen oder Körbe sind sehr praktisch, um schnell und einfach Spielzeuge aufzubewahren, und die Kinder daran zu gewöhnen, die Sachen aufzuräumen, wenn sie mit dem Spielen aufgehört haben.

Dozen of manden zijn praktisch om speelgoed snel op te bergen en om kinderen te leren om na het spelen hun speelgoed op te ruimen.

Las cajas o cestos son muy prácticos para guardar de una manera rápida y fácil los juguetes, y acostumbrar a los niños a dejar las cosas en su sitio cuando terminan de jugar.

Le scatole o i cesti sono molto comodi per riporre in modo facile e veloce i giochi, abituando i bambini a mettere a posto al termine del momento di gioco.

As caixas ou cestos são soluções práticas para guardar de forma rápida e fácil os brinquedos e habituar as crianças a deixar as coisas no respectivo sítio quando acabam de brincar.

Lådor och korgar är mycket praktiska för att enkelt och lätt städa undan leksaker och för att lära barnen att plocka undan efter sig när de lekt färdigt.

In large, shared bedrooms divide the space with partitions to define the sleeping area from the study and play areas.

Vous pouvez distribuer l'espace des chambres partagées et très grandes à l'aide de cloisons qui délimitent le coin repos, l'espace de travail et le coin jeu.

In sehr großen Zimmern, die sich die Kinder teilen, trennen Sie den Raum durch Trennwände, um den Schlafbereich von dem Lern- und Spielbereich zu trennen.

In gedeelde en heel grote slaapkamers kunt u de ruimte indelen met tussenschotten om het slaapgedeelte van het studeer- en speelgedeelte af te scheiden.

En dormitorios compartidos y muy grandes divide el espacio con tabiques para distinguir la zona de descanso, de la de estudio y la de juego.

Nelle camere in cui dormono più bambini e di grandi dimensioni, segmenta lo spazio con divisori per differenziare la zona notte dallo studio e dall'area di gioco.

Em quartos partilhados e de grande dimensão, delimite o espaço com divisórias para distinguir entre a zona de descanso, a de estudo e a de brincar.

I stora sovrum som delas av flera barn kan man dela upp utrymmet med mellanväggar i viloområde, studieområde och lekområde.

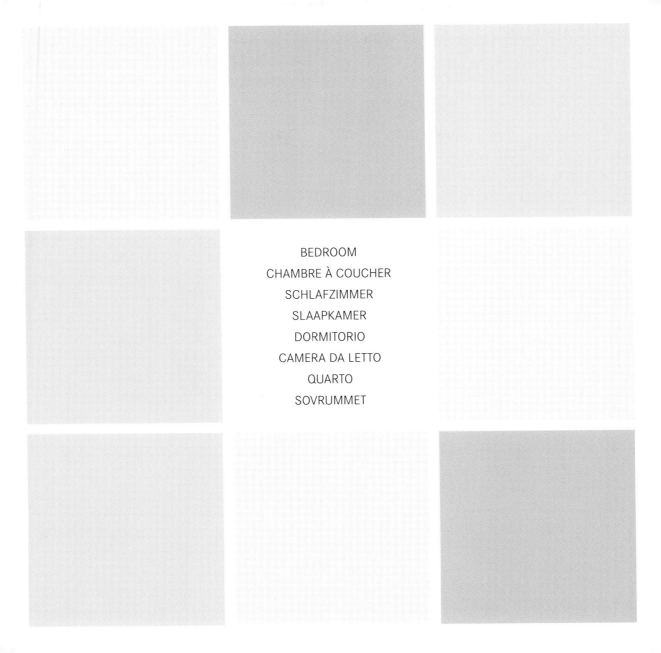

BEDROOM

CHAMBRE À COUCHER

SCHLAFZIMMER

SLAAPKAMER

DORMITORIO

CAMERA DA LETTO

QUARTO

SOVRUMMET

A square shelf hanging over the side of the bed is a bedside table that takes up very little space and is visually very light.

Une planche carrée saillante montée à côté du lit devient une table de nuit qui occupe très peu de place et apporte visuellement une grande légèreté.

Ein freischwebendes quadratisches Regalbrett an der Bettseite dient als Nachttisch, der sehr wenig Platz einnimmt und sehr leicht aussieht.

Een zwevende vierkante plank naast het bed is een nachtkastje dat weinig ruimte inneemt en tegelijkertijd visueel licht is.

Una balda cuadrada en voladizo al costado de la cama es una mesilla de noche que ocupa muy poco espacio y resulta visualmente muy liviana.

Una mensola quadrata sospesa accanto al letto è un comodino che occupa pochissimo spazio e risulta visivamente molto leggero.

Uma prateleira quadrada suspensa fixa às costas da cama é uma mesa-de-cabeceira que ocupa muito pouco espaço e visualmente é muito leve.

En fyrkantig utspringande hylla vid sidan av sängen är ett alternativ till sängbord som tar upp mycket lite plats och som visuellt är mycket lätt.

If there is a setback in the wall, create a built-in baseboard-headboard that serves as a shelf, perfect to support the table lamp.

Si le mur présente un décrochement, une tête de lit en maçonnerie fait office d'étagère et est idéale pour poser des lampes de table.

Wenn sich eine Nische in der Wand befindet, bauen Sie einen Sockel, der als Ablage dient und einen idealen Platz für die Nachtischlampe bietet.

Als de muur een inspringend gedeelte heeft, creëer dan een gemetselde sokkel-hoofdeinde die dienst doet als schap, ideaal om de tafellamp op te zetten.

Si en la pared hay un retranqueo, crea un zócalo-cabecero de obra que funcione como estante, ideal para apoyar la lámpara de mesa.

Se sulla parete c'è un rientro, crea uno zoccolo-testata in muratura da utilizzare come ripiano, ideale per appoggiare la luce del comodino.

Caso existam reentrâncias na parede, crie um rodapé-cabeceira de alvenaria que funcione como estante, ideal para apoiar o candeeiro de mesa.

Om den finns en inbyggnad i väggen kan du skapa en specialbyggd sänggavelslist som även fungerar som hylla där man kan placera en läslampa.

If you do not have a bedside table or it is very small, install a lighting fixture that hangs from the ceiling close to the height of the bed.

Si vous ne disposez pas de table de nuit ou si elle est très petite, vous accrochez une lampe au plafond et vous la faites descendre à proximité du lit.

Wenn Sie keinen Nachttisch haben oder dieser sehr klein ist, installieren Sie eine tief hängende Deckenlampe nahe am Bett.

Heeft u geen nachtkastje of is die heel klein, verlicht dan met een wandlamp die laag vanaf het plafond op een hoogte dichtbij het bed schijnt.

Si no tienes mesilla de noche o es muy pequeña, ilumina con un aplique que baja desde el techo a una altura muy cercana a la cama.

Se non hai un comodino o se è molto piccolo, per illuminare usa un'applique che scende dal soffitto a un'altezza molto vicina al letto.

Caso não tenha uma mesa-de-cabeceira ou se a mesma for muito pequena, para a iluminação utilize um aplique que desça desde o tecto até uma altura muito próxima da cama.

Om du inte har något sängbord eller om det är mycket litet, kan du ordna belysning med en spotlight i taket som hänger strax ovanför sängen.

Create a built-in shelf on the wall. To reduce its weight and make the room seem more uncluttered, paint the inside and back of the shelf the same color as the wall.

On peut construire dans le mur une étagère en maçonnerie. Pour qu'elle paraisse plus légère et pour mieux dégager la pièce, on peut peindre son intérieur et le fond de la même couleur que le mur.

Bauen Sie eine Ablage in die Wand ein. Um deren Gewicht zu verringern und damit das Zimmer geräumiger wirkt, streichen Sie sie innen und den Hintergrund in derselben Farbe wie die Wand.

Bevestig een gemetselde plank aan de muur. Om het gewicht te verminderen en de slaapkamer opgeruimder te laten lijken kunt u de binnenkant en achterkant in dezelfde kleur als de muur schilderen.

Crea sobre la pared una repisa de obra. Para disminuir su peso y hacer la habitación más despejada, pinta su interior y el fondo del mismo color que la pared.

Crea sopra la parete un vano in muratura. Per diminuirne l'impatto e rendere più "pulita" la stanza, piuttura l'interno e il fondo dello stesso colore della parete.

Crie sobre a parede uma prateleira de alvenaria. Para diminuir o seu impacto e tornar o quarto mais amplo, pinte o interior da prateleira e o fundo da mesma cor que a parede.

Sätt en inbyggd hylla på väggen. För att ge ett lättare intryck bör den målas i samma färg som väggen.

Wall-mounted lights by the bed are perfect to save space on the bedside table and provide very specific lighting for reading.

Les appliques murales à côté du lit libèrent les tables de nuit et apportent un éclairage très adapté à la lecture.

Mit ein paar Wandlampen beim Bett gewinnt man Platz auf dem Nachttisch und gutes Leselicht.

Met wandlampen naast het bed krijgt u meer ruimte op het nachttafeltje en een handige leeslamp.

Con unos apliques de pared junto a la cama, se gana espacio en la mesilla de noche y una iluminación muy puntual para la lectura.

Con delle applique da parete accanto al letto è possibile guadagnare spazio sul comodino e disporre di un'illuminazione più concentrata per la lettura.

Com uns apliques de parede junto à cama, ganha espaço na mesa-de-cabeceira e uma iluminação muito esporádica para leitura.

Med inbyggda spotlights bredvid sängen får man mer plats på sängbordet och en riktad belysning för läsning.

So that the radiator does not get in the way, build a bespoke unit around it.

Le radiateur ne doit pas empêcher d'installer des éléments contre le mur. Il peut être intégré dans un meuble sur mesure.

Damit der Heizkörper das Aufstellen von Möbeln an der Wand nicht behindert, konstruieren Sie ein Möbelstück nach Maß um ihn herum.

Laat de radiator geen belemmering zijn om meubels tegen de muur te zetten. Maak een meubelstuk op maat waar de radiator wordt ingebouwd.

Que el radiador no sea un impedimento para situar muebles en la pared. Construye un mueble a medida que lo incorpore.

Il radiatore non deve impedire l'aggiunta di mobili a parete. Realizza un mobile su misura per includerlo.

Não permita que o aquecedor seja um impedimento para a colocação de móveis na parede. Construa um móvel à medida que o incorpore.

Elementet bör inte vara ett hinder för att placera möbler vid väggen. Låt bygga en möbel som insluter det.

Increase the storage capacity of the closet with a half height extension that also defines a dressing area.

La capacité de rangement de l'armoire peut être augmentée avec un meuble supplémentaire de hauteur moyenne servant aussi à délimiter un espace pour le dressing.

Erweitern Sie die den Platz im Schrank durch einen Anbau in halber Höhe, der zudem dazu dient, einen Umkleideraum abzugrenzen.

Vergroot de opbergcapaciteit van de kledingkast met een half zo hoog verlengstuk dat bovendien een kleedruimte kan afbakenen.

Amplía la capacidad de almacenaje del armario con una extensión a media altura que además sirve para definir un espacio de vestidor.

Aumenta le capacità di contenimento xdell'armadio con un'estensione a metà altezza che serva anche per definire uno spazio guardaroba.

Amplie a capacidade de arrumação do armário com uma extensão a meia altura que sirva também para definir um espaço para vestir.

Öka garderobens förvaringskapacitet med en utökning vid halvhög höjd som dessutom fungerar för att göra en påklädningsutrymme.

Replace the overhead lighting for several, different points of light to create a cozy atmosphere in the bedroom.

L'éclairage zénithal peut être remplacé par différents points de lumière créant une ambiance accueillante dans la chambre.

Ersetzen Sie das Deckenlicht durch mehrere verschiedene Lichtquellen, um eine gemütliche Atmosphäre im Schlafzimmer zu schaffen.

Vervang verlichting van bovenaf door verschillende lichtpunten om de slaapkamer gezelliger te maken.

Sustituye la iluminación cenital por varios y diferentes puntos de luz para crear un ambiente acogedor en el dormitorio.

Sostituisci l'illuminazione zenitale con punti luce diversificati per creare un ambiente accogliente in camera.

Substitua a iluminação central por vários e diferentes pontos de luz para criar um ambiente acolhedor no quarto.

Ersätt ljuset från takfönstret med flera olika ljuskällor för att skapa en hemtrevlig atmosfär i sovrummet.

Take full advantage of all the walls of the room. Install a shelf on the wall of the headboard and hide it behind the curtains.

Vous pouvez exploiter au maximum le potentiel des murs de la pièce : cette bibliothèque installée derrière la tête de lit est cachée par des rideaux.

Nutzen Sie alle Wände des Zimmers so gut wie möglich aus. Stellen Sie ein Regal an der Wand am Kopfende des Bettes auf, und verstecken Sie es hinter Gardinen.

Benut alle wanden van de slaapkamer maximaal. Installeer een wandmeubel aan de muur van het hoofdeinde van het bed en verberg deze achter een gordijn.

Saca el máximo provecho de todas las paredes de la habitación. Instala una estantería en la pared de la cabecera de la cama y escóndela detrás de unas cortinas.

Sfrutta al massimo tutte le pareti della stanza. Monta una scaffalatura sulla parete della testata del letto nascondendola dietro delle tende.

Tire o máximo proveito de todas as paredes do quarto. Instale uma estante na parede da cabeceira da cama e esconda-a atrás de umas cortinas.

Utnyttja sovrummets väggar maximalt. Placera en hylla vid sängens huvudända och göm den bakom några gardiner.

Create a large wardrobe in one corner of the bedroom with a set of shelves behind a semicircular curtain rail.

On peut créer une grande armoire dans un coin de la chambre avec des étagères posées derrière des rideaux accrochés à une tringle en quart de cercle.

Konstruieren Sie einen großen Schrank in einer Ecke des Schlafzimmers durch ein Regal, das sich hinter einem Vorhang an einer halbkreisförmigen Schiene befindet.

Maak een ruime kast in een hoek van de slaapkamer door een wandmeubel achter een gordijn in halfronde rail te zetten.

Crea un armario amplio en un rincón del dormitorio con una estantería situada detrás de una cortina en riel semicircular.

Crea un ampio armadio in un angolo della camera con uno scaffale posto dietro una tenda con guida semicircolare.

Crie um armário amplo numa zona do quarto com uma estante situada atrás de uma cortina com calha semicircular.

Gör en rymlig garderob i ett hörn av sovrummet med en hylla bakom ett skynke i en halvcirkelformad skärm.

Use boxes to maintain order. It doesn't matter what is visible, especially if it has an attractive design in keeping with the decor of the bedroom.

Les boîtes permettent de ranger correctement les affaires. Elles peuvent être visibles, surtout si elles ont des dessins attrayants en accord avec la décoration de la chambre.

Greifen Sie zu Schachteln, um Ordnung zu halten. Es macht nichts, dass man sie sieht, vor allem, wenn sie ein attraktives Design haben, das zu der Einrichtung des Schlafzimmers passt.

Gebruik dozen om de slaapkamer opgeruimd te houden. Het geeft niet dat ze in het zicht staan, vooral niet als ze een aantrekkelijk design hebben dat overeenstemt met de inrichting van de slaapkamer.

Recurre a las cajas para mantener el orden. No importa que queden a la vista, sobre todo si tienen un diseño atractivo acorde con la decoración del dormitorio.

Utilizza le scatole per tenere in ordine. Non importa se restano visibili, soprattutto se hanno una fantasia piacevole in sintonia con gli arredi della camera.

Recorra a caixas para manter a ordem. Não importa que fiquem à vista, sobretudo se tiverem um design atractivo que se enquadre na decoração do quarto.

Använd lådor för att hålla ordning. Det gör inget om de är synliga, speciellt inte om de har en attraktiv design som passar sovrummets inredning.

Place a pair of footrests with storage space at the foot of the bed to be able to dress yourself comfortably and have extra space to store blankets.

Vous pouvez poser deux repose-pieds avec coffre de rangement au pied du lit : ils seront utiles au moment de vous habiller et fourniront un espace supplémentaire pour stocker les couvertures.

Stellen Sie zwei Fußstützen, in denen man Dinge aufbewahren kann, am Fußende des Bettes auf, damit Sie sich bequem anziehen können und einen zusätzlichen Platz für die Aufbewahrung der Decken haben.

Plaats enkele bankjes met opbergruimte aan de voet van het bed, zodat u zich comfortabel kunt aankleden en over extra ruimte beschikt om dekens te bewaren.

Coloca un par de reposapiés con espacio de almacenamiento a los pies de la cama para vestirte cómodamente y contar con un espacio extra donde guardar las mantas.

Sistema un paio di poggiapiedi-contenitori ai piedi del letto per vestirti comodamente e disporre di uno spazio aggiuntivo in cui riporre le coperte.

Coloque um par de apoios de pés com espaço para arrumação aos pés da cama para que se possa vestir comodamente e dispor de espaço extra onde guardar as mantas.

Placera ett par fotpallar med förvaringsutrymme vid sängens fotända. På så sätt kan du klä på dig enklare och du kan även förvara filtar där.

Incorporate the bathroom into the bedroom through a built-in bath that can be converted into a bench using a wooden lid.

La salle de bain peut être intégrée à la chambre : la baignoire en maçonnerie se transforme en banquette grâce à une planche en bois.

Integrieren Sie das Bad ins Schlafzimmer mit einer eingebauten Badewanne, die sich dank eines Holzdeckels in eine Bank verwandelt.

Integreer de badkamer in de slaapkamer door middel van een ingemetseld bad dat kan worden omgevormd tot bank met een houten afdekplaat.

Integra el baño en el dormitorio a través de una bañera de obra que se convierte en banco gracias a una tapa de madera.

Integra bagno e camera inserendo una vasca in muratura che si trasforma in panca grazie a una chiusura di legno.

Integre a casa de banho no quarto utilizando uma banheira de alvenaria que possa ser convertida num banco através de uma tampa de madeira.

Integrera badrummet i sovrummet med ett inbyggt badkar som förvandlas till bänk med en träskiva.

Save space and put part of the bathroom in the bedroom. It is important that the washbowl and vanity unit have the same style as the rest of the bedroom.

Si on optimise l'espace en intégrant une partie de la salle de bain dans la chambre, le lavabo et son meuble seront du même style que les autres éléments de la pièce.

Gewinnen Sie Platz, indem Sie einen Teil des Bades im Schlafzimmer installieren. Es ist wichtig, dass das Waschbecken und der Waschtisch im selben Stil wie das übrige Schlafzimmer gehalten sind.

Verkrijg meer ruimte en plaats een deel van de badkamer in de slaapkamer. Het is belangrijk dat de wastafel en het meubelstuk daaronder dezelfde stijl hebben als die van de rest van de slaapkamer.

Gana espacio y coloca una parte del baño en la habitación. Es importante que el lavamanos y el mueble encimero tengan el mismo estilo que el resto del dormitorio.

Guadagna spazio e sistema una parte del bagno in camera. È importante che lavamano e mobile del bagno abbiano lo stesso stile del resto della camera.

Permite ganhar espaço e coloque uma parte da casa de banho no quarto. É importante que o lavatório e o móvel de apoio tenham o mesmo estilo que o resto do quarto.

Få mer utrymme och placera en del av badrummet i sovrummet. Det är viktigt att handfatet och möbeln har samma stil som resten av sovrummet.

Ideally, a faucet attached to the wall is ideal for small washbasins. You can save space and there is no water spray.

Le robinet sortant directement du mur est la solution idéale pour les petits lavabos. Il gagne de la place et évite les éclaboussures.

Ideal für kleine Waschbecken ist ein Wasserhahn, der direkt aus der Wand kommt. Er spart Platz und verspritzt kein Wasser.

Ideaal voor kleine wastafels is een kraan die rechtstreeks uit de muur komt. Hierdoor wordt ruimte bespaard en voorkomt u waterspetters.

Lo ideal para lavamanos pequeños es un grifo que sale directamente de la pared. Ahorra espacio y no salpica agua.

Nel caso di lavelli piccoli, la soluzione ideale è un rubinetto applicato direttamente sulla parete. Consente di risparmiare spazio e non causa schizzi di acqua.

O ideal para lavatórios pequenos é uma torneira que saia directamente da parede. Poupa espaço e não salpica água.

För små handfat är det bäst med en kran som sitter direkt i väggen. Det sparar utrymme och ger mindre vattenstänk.

Create a harmonious environment in the bedroom using fabrics with the same range of colors and patterns. Smooth textiles are easier to combine.

Les tissus appartenant à la même gamme de couleurs et d'imprimés créent une atmosphère harmonieuse dans la chambre. Les tissus unis sont plus faciles à associer.

Schaffen Sie im Schlafzimmer mit Textilien derselben Farb- und Musterskala eine harmonische Atmosphäre. Einfarbige Textilien kann man leichter kombinieren.

Zorg voor een harmonieuze sfeer in de slaapkamer met textiel in hetzelfde kleurengamma en bedrukte stof. Effen stoffen zijn gemakkelijker te combineren.

Crea un ambiente armónico en el dormitorio a partir de textiles de la misma gama de tonos y estampados. Los textiles lisos son más fáciles de combinar.

Crea un ambiente armonico in camera partendo dai tessuti nella stessa gamma di colori e stampe. I tessuti lisci sono più facili da combinare.

Crie um ambiente de harmonia no quarto utilizando têxteis da mesma gama de tons e estampados. Os têxteis lisos são mais fáceis de combinar.

Skapa en harmonisk atmosfär i sovrummet med textilier i samma färgnyanser och mönster. Enfärgade textilier är enklare att kombinera.

Double-height houses are ideal for a bedroom in the mezzanine. For increased privacy, place a small wall on the side that is connected to the rest of the house.

Les maisons sur deux niveaux sont idéales pour installer la chambre à coucher dans la mezzanine. Un muret du côté communicant avec le reste de la maison vous aidera à préserver votre intimité.

Die Häuser von doppelter Höhe sind ideal für den Einbau des Schlafzimmers im Halbgeschoss. Für mehr Privatsphäre bringen Sie an der Seite, die es mit der übrigen Wohnung verbindet, eine niedrige Mauer an.

Huizen met twee hoogtes zijn ideaal om de slaapkamer op de tussenverdieping in te richten. Plaats voor meer privacy een muurtje aan de kant die in verbinding staat met de rest van de woning.

Las casas de doble altura son ideales para instalar el dormitorio en el entresuelo. Para una mayor privacidad, coloca un murete en el lado que comunica con el resto de la casa.

Le case con doppia altezza sono ideali per sistemare la camera nel mezzanino. Per maggiore privacy, sistema un muretto sul lato che comunica con il resto della casa.

As casas de dupla altura são ideais para a instalação do quarto no nível superior. Para uma maior privacidade, coloque um muro no lado que comunica com o resto da casa.

I hus med dubbel höjd är det idealiskt att placera sovrummet på mellanvåningen. För att få det mer ostört kan man placera en liten mur på den sidan som leder till resten av huset.

Who said the bed had to be stuck to the wall? If you have enough space leave an area around the bed so you can walk around it.

Qui a dit que le lit doit être toujours contre le mur ? Si vous avez suffisamment de place, vous pouvez laisser de l'espace autour de ce meuble pour faciliter la circulation.

Wer sagt, dass das Bett immer an der Wand stehen muss? Wenn der Raum groß genug ist, lassen Sie Platz frei, um leichter um dieses Möbelstück herumgehen zu können.

Wie zegt dat het bed altijd tegen de muur moet staan? Heeft u voldoende ruimte, laat dan loopruimte open rondom het bed.

¿Quién dijo que la cama debe estar siempre contra la pared? Si cuentas con superficie suficiente deja un espacio para circular más fácilmente alrededor de este mueble.

Chi ha detto che il letto deve stare sempre addossato alla parete? Se c'è spazio sufficiente, lascia uno spazio per passarvi più facilmente intorno.

Quem disse que a cama deve estar sempre encostada à parede? Caso disponha de área suficiente reserve espaço para circular mais facilmente em redor deste móvel.

Vem har sagt att sängen måste stå mot väggen? Om du har tillräckligt med plats kan du lämna plats runt möbeln så att man kan röra sig runt den.

A bespoke piece of furniture has two uses such as this unit that can be used as a chest of drawers and a bed.

Ce meuble sur mesure a une double fonction : celle d'armoire ou commode et de lit.

Geben Sie einem einzigen maßgefertigten Möbelstück zwei Verwendungszwecke, wie diesem, das als Schrank oder Kommode und als Bett dient.

Gebruik een op maat gemaakt meubelstuk voor twee doeleinden, zoals deze, die dienst doet als kledingkast en als bed.

Da dos utilidades a un solo mueble hecho a medida, como este, que sirve como armario o cómoda y cama.

Un unico mobile realizzato su misura può avere una doppia funzione, come questo che serve sia da armadio che da letto.

Atribua duas utilidades a um único móvel feito à medida, como este que serve de armário ou cómoda e cama.

En måttbeställd möbel kan ha flera olika användningsområden, som denna som fungerar både som skåp eller byrå och säng.

Build a platform at a distinct height to create a relaxation area and make use of the space for low closet space.

Comment construire une plateforme à une hauteur différente pour créer une zone de repos et profiter de l'espace vide pour installer des armoires basses.

Errichten Sie eine Plattform in einer gewissen Höhe, um dort einen Ruhebereich zu schaffen und die Lücke für niedrige Schränke auszunutzen.

Bouw een platform op een bepaalde hoogte voor een ontspanningsruimte en benut de opening voor lage kasten.

Construye una plataforma a una altura bien diferenciada para crear allí una zona de relax y aprovechar el hueco para armarios bajos.

Costruisci una piattaforma a un'altezza ben differenziata per creare una zona relax e sfruttare il vano sottostante per inserire degli armadi bassi

Construa uma plataforma a uma altura bem diferenciada para criar ali uma zona de descontracção e aproveite o vão para armários baixos.

Bygg en plattform på en annan höjd än resten av rummet och skapa en relaxavdelning där. Utnyttja tomrummet under för låga garderober.

Create a different space with a built-in bed or a mattress placed directly on an oriental style ground level platform.

Vous pouvez créer un espace différent avec un lit en maçonnerie ou installer le matelas sur un dénivelé à l'oriental, c'est-à-dire à même le sol.

Schaffen Sie einen besonderen Raum mit einem eingebauten Bett oder legen Sie die Matratze im orientalischen Stil auf ein Podest direkt auf den Boden.

Creëer een originele ruimte met een gemetselde bad, of leg de matras direct op een verhoging vlak boven de grond, in oosterse stijl.

Crea un espacio diferente con una cama de obra, o sitúa directamente el colchón sobre un desnivel a ras del suelo, al estilo oriental.

Crea uno spazio diverso con un letto in muratura oppure posiziona direttamente il materasso a terra, su una porzione di pavimento rialzata, in stile orientale.

Crie um espaço diferente com uma cama de alvenaria, ou coloque directamente o colchão sobre um desnível rente ao solo, ao estilo oriental.

Skapa en annorlunda plats med en specialbyggd säng eller placera madrassen direkt på en upphöjning i golvet, på orientaliskt vis.

In a loft, install large format panels to increase privacy in the bedroom.

Dans un loft, des panneaux de grandes dimensions préservent l'intimité de la chambre à coucher.

In einem *loft* installieren Sie großformatige Wandplatten, um dem Schlafzimmer Privatsphäre zu verleihen.

Installeer in een *loft* panelen van groot formaat voor meer privacy in de slaapkamer.

En un *loft*, instala unos paneles de gran formato para dar privacidad al dormitorio.

In un *loft* installa dei grandi pannelli per trasmettere privacy alla camera.

Num *loft*, instale painéis de grande dimensão para dar privacidade ao quarto.

I en loftvåning kan man installera några stora skärmar för att ge sovrummet avskildhet.

A linear photo arrangement is perfect to decorate a wall behind a bed without a headboard.

Une composition de photos alignées est parfaite pour décorer le mur auquel le lit est adossé et permet de se passer de la tête de lit.

Eine Reihe von Fotos in einer Linie aufgehängt, ist perfekt, um die Wand, an der das Bett steht, zu dekorieren, wenn man auf das Kopfteil verzichtet.

Een compositie van foto's op een rechte lijn is perfect om de muur waartegen het bed staat te versieren en af te zien van een hoofdeinde.

Una composición en línea de fotos es perfecta para decorar la pared en la que se apoya la cama y prescindir del cabecero.

Una composizione con foto allineate è perfetta per arricchire la parete su cui appoggia il letto e consente di fare a meno della testata.

Uma composição alinhada de fotografias é perfeita para decorar a parede na qual está apoiada a cama e prescindir da cabeceira.

En komposition av foton placerade i en linje är perfekt för att dekorera väggen som sängen står emot. På så sätt behövs ingen sänggavel.

A metal rail and shelf structure, plus a drawer on wheels is enough to create a reasonable closet space.

Une structure métallique avec étagères, penderie et meuble à tiroirs sur roulettes suffit à créer une grande armoire.

Eine Metallstruktur mit Stange und Regalbrett und ein Schubladenschrank mit Rädern genügen, um einen Schrank mit beträchtlichem Fassungsvermögen zu schaffen.

Een metalen structuur met een stang en plank naast een ladenkast op wieltjes is voldoende om een kledingkast met behoorlijke inhoud te creëren.

Una estructura metálica con barra y estante, más una cajonera con ruedas, es suficiente para crear un armario de capacidad considerable.

Una struttura metallica con appendiabiti e ripiano, oltre a una cassettiera con ruote, basta per creare un armadio piuttosto capiente.

Uma estrutura metálica com cabide e estante, mais uma cómoda com rodas, é o suficiente para criar um armário com capacidade considerável.

En metallstruktur med en stång och en hylla, samt en låda med hjul, är tillräckligt för att skapa en garderob med stor förvaringskapacitet.

DINING ROOM

SALLE À MANGER

ESSZIMMER

EETKAMER

COMEDOR

SALA DA PRANZO

SALA DE JANTAR

MATSALEN

Another way to define the dining area is by choosing furniture in a color that makes the space stand out.

Une autre manière pour délimiter la salle à manger consiste à choisir des meubles d'une couleur qui se détache des autres.

Eine andere Art, den Essplatz abzugrenzen, ist, das Mobiliar in einer Farbe zu wählen, die sich von der Umgebung abhebt.

Een andere manier om de eetkamer af te bakenen is om te kiezen voor meubilair in een kleur die opvalt in de ruimte.

Otra manera de definir el espacio del comedor es mediante la elección de un mobiliario de un color que destaque en el ambiente.

Un altro modo di definire lo spazio della sala da pranzo è tramite la scelta di arredi in un colore che si imponga nell'ambiente.

Outra maneira de definir a sala de jantar é através da escolha de mobiliário de uma cor que se destaque no espaço.

Ett annat sätt att definiera matsalen är att välja möbler i en färg som skiljer sig från omgivningen.

Chairs do not have to have the same style as the table.
Be adventurous with contrasting textures and shapes to
create a unique and cozy dining room.

Les chaises ne doivent pas forcément être dans le
même style que la table : vous pouvez oser et créer des
contrastes de matériaux et de formes donnant vie à une
salle à manger à la fois personnelle et accueillante.

Die Stühle müssen nicht unbedingt denselben Stil wie der
Tisch haben. Seien Sie wagemutig mit kontrastierenden
Materialien und Formen, um einen so persönlichen wie
gemütlichen Essplatz einzurichten.

De stoelen hoeven niet persé dezelfde stijl als de tafel
te hebben. Durf te spelen met contrasten in texturen en
vormen, voor een zowel persoonlijke als gezellige eetkamer.

No es obligatorio que las sillas sean del mismo estilo que
la mesa. Atrévete con los contrastes de texturas y formas
para crear un comedor tan personal como acogedor.

Non è obbligatorio che le sedie siano combinate con il
tavolo. Azzarda optando per materiali e forme contrastanti
per creare una sala da pranzo personale e accogliente.

As cadeiras não têm que ser obrigatoriamente do mesmo
estilo que a mesa. Seja arrojado com o contraste de
texturas e formas para criar uma área de refeições tão
pessoal como acolhedora.

Stolarna måste inte nödvändigtvis vara i samma stil som
bordet. Våga blanda konstrasterande texturer och former
för att skapa en matsal som är både personlig
och inbjudande.

A round table is ideal for saving space when you don't have much of it.

Une table ronde est la solution idéale pour gagner de la place lorsque les mètres carrés de la salle à manger manquent.

Ein runder Tisch ist ideal, um Platz zu sparen, wenn das Esszimmer klein ist.

Een ronde tafel is ideaal om ruimte te creëren in een kleine eetkamer.

Una mesa redonda resulta ideal para ganar espacio cuando los metros del comedor son escasos.

Un tavolo rotondo è la soluzione ideale per guadagnare spazio quando i metri quadrati della sala da pranzo sono pochi.

Uma mesa redonda é a opção ideal para ganhar espaço quando os metros da área de refeições são escassos.

Ett runt bord är idealiskt för att få mer plats när matsalen är begränsad.

Opt for an extendable table that can be opened out easily so that the dining room can adapt to the number of guests.

Une table à rallonge avec un système d'ouverture simple permet d'adapter la salle à manger aux repas avec des invités.

Stellen Sie einen Ausziehtisch mit einem einfachen Ausziehmechanismus auf, damit der Essplatz für Essen mit Gästen angepasst werden kann.

Installeer een uittrekbare tafel met een eenvoudig uittreksysteem zodat de eetkamer kan worden aangepast als er gasten komen eten.

Instala una mesa extensible con un sistema de apertura cómodo para que el comedor se adapte a las comidas con invitados.

Inserisci un tavolo allungabile dotato di pratico sistema di apertura affinché la sala da pranzo si adatti al numero di ospiti.

Instale uma mesa extensível com um sistema de abertura cómodo para que o espaço se adapte às refeições com convidados.

Installera ett utdragbart bord med ett enkelt förlängningssystem som gör att matsalen kan anpassas till antal gäster.

Instead of a large, strong table that takes up the center of the room, use two small tables that can be joined together for more flexibility.

Remplacer une table grande et massive qui remplit la partie centrale de la salle à manger par deux petites tables pouvant s'unir donne une plus grande flexibilité.

An Stelle eines großen, massiven Tisches, der das gesamte Zentrum des Essbereiches einnimmt, stellen Sie zwei kleine Tische, die man zusammenstellen kann. Damit gewinnen Sie Flexibilität.

Installeer, in plaats van een grote, massieve tafel die de centrale ruimte van de eetkamer in beslag neemt, twee kleine tafels die aan elkaar kunnen worden geschoven, voor meer flexibiliteit.

En lugar de una mesa grande y maciza que llena el espacio central del comedor, instala dos mesas pequeñas que se puedan unir y ganarás flexibilidad.

Al posto di un grande tavolo in legno massiccio che satura lo spazio centrale della sala da pranzo, opta per due tavoli piccoli che possano essere uniti e otterrai una soluzione flessibile.

Em vez de uma mesa grande e pesada que ocupe a zona central do espaço, instale duas mesas pequenas que possam ser unidas de forma a ganhar flexibilidade.

Istället för ett stort, kompakt bord som fyller matsalens centrala del kan man installera två små bord som kan sättas ihop. På så sätt blir det mer flexibelt.

Opt for designer chairs a different color from the table so that they stand out and define the style of the dining room.

Le choix de chaises qui diffèrent de la table par leur dessin et par leur couleur en fait le point de mire de la salle à manger et définit son style.

Wählen Sie Stühle in einem vom Tisch unterschiedenen Design und anderer, damit sie die Hauptrolle spielen und den Stil des Essplatzes bestimmen.

Kies design stoelen in een andere kleur dan de tafel, zodat ze het middelpunt vormen en bepalend zijn voor de stijl van de eetkamer.

Selecciona sillas de diseño y color diferente a la mesa para que se conviertan en protagonistas y definan el estilo del comedor.

Scegli delle sedie di design e colore diverso da abbinare con il tavolo affinché abbiano un ruolo di protagoniste e definiscano lo stile della sala da pranzo.

Seleccione cadeiras com design e cor diferentes da mesa para que se convertam em protagonistas e definam o estilo da sala de jantar.

Välj stolar i en design och färg som skiljer sig från bordet så att de får uppmärksamhet och bestämmer matsalens stil.

For an elegant meal with guests, use one or two ranges of colors and materials that blend together.

Pour un repas élégant avec des invités, vous ne choisirez qu'une ou deux gammes de couleurs et des éléments qui vont ensemble.

Für ein elegantes Essen mit Gästen verwenden Sie nur eine oder zwei Farbskalen und Materialien, die zueinander passen.

Gebruik, voor een elegant etentje met gasten, slechts een of twee kleurengamma's en materialen die onderling combineren.

Para una comida elegante con invitados, utiliza una o dos gamas de colores solamente y materiales que combinen entre sí.

Per un pranzo o una cena elegante con invitati, usa solo una o due gamme di colori e materiali combinabili tra loro.

Para uma refeição elegante com convidados, utilize somente uma ou duas gamas de cores e materiais que combinem bem entre si.

För en elegant måltid med gäster bör du bara använda en eller två färgnyanser och material som passar ihop.

A classic way to integrate the dining room into the living room is using the same materials for the furniture and in particular the same range of colors.

Une manière classique pour intégrer la salle à manger au salon consiste à choisir les mêmes matériaux pour le mobilier et tout particulièrement, la même gamme de couleurs.

Eine klassische Art, den Essplatz in das Wohnzimmer zu integrieren ist, dieselben Materialien und vor allem dieselbe Farbskala für das Mobiliar zu verwenden.

Een klassieke manier om de eetkamer in de zitkamer te integreren is door gebruik te maken van dezelfde materialen voor het meubilair en met name hetzelfde kleurenkleurengamma.

Una forma clásica de integrar el comedor al salón es utilizando los mismos materiales para el mobiliario y especialmente la misma gama de colores.

Un modo classico di integrare la sala da pranzo con il salotto è quello di utilizzare gli stessi materiali per gli arredi, e soprattutto la stessa gamma di colori.

Uma forma clássica de integrar a área de refeições na sala é utilizando os mesmos materiais para o mobiliário e especialmente a mesma gama de cores.

Ett klassiskt sätt att integrera matsalen i vardagsrummet är att använda samma material i möblerna och samma färgskala.

If the table is long, fit at least two equidistant lamps.

Si la table est longue, il faut installer au moins deux plafonniers équidistants.

Wenn der Tisch lang ist, sollte man wenigstens zwei Hängelampen im gleichen Abstand installieren.

Als de tafel lang is moeten er tenminste twee plafondlampen worden opgehangen, op gelijke afstand van elkaar.

Si la mesa es larga, se deben instalar al menos dos lámparas de techo equidistantes.

Se il tavolo è lungo, aggiungere almeno due lampadari a soffitto, equidistanti l'uno dall'altro.

Se a mesa for comprida, deverão ser instalados pelo menos dois candeeiros de tecto equidistantes.

Om bordet är långt bör man ha minst två taklampor på jämt avstånd.

To create a colonial-style dining room choose natural looking wooden table and chairs in white, with natural fiber elements.

Vous pouvez créer une salle à manger de style colonial avec de chaises et une table en bois naturel ou patinées en blanc, avec des éléments en fibres naturelles.

Für einen Essplatz im Kolonialstil suchen Sie Tisch und Stühle aus Naturholz oder weiß gestrichen mit Elementen aus Naturfaser aus.

Zoek, om een eetkamer in koloniale stijl in te richten, stoelen en een tafel van natuurlijk of wit gelakt hout, met elementen van natuurvezel.

Para crear un comedor de estilo colonial busca sillas y mesa de madera natural o patinada en blanco, con elementos de fibras naturales.

Per creare una sala da pranzo in stile coloniale, cerca sedie e tavolo in legno naturale o patinato di bianco, con elementi di fibre naturali.

Para criar uma sala de jantar de estilo colonial procure cadeiras e mesa de madeira natural ou com aplicação de pátina em branco, com elementos de fibras naturais.

För att skapa en matsal i kolonialstil kan du leta efter stolar och bord i naturträ eller med vit patina, med inslag av naturfiber.

A contemporary dining room integrates wood and metal furniture with a sleek design.

Una salle à manger de style contemporain mélange des meubles en bois et en métal au dessin épuré.

Ein Essplatz in modernem Stil besteht aus einer Kombination von Möbeln aus Holz und Metall mit klarem Design.

Een eetkamer in eigentijdse stijl vormt een eenheid door houten en metalen meubels met een verfijnd ontwerp.

Un comedor de estilo contemporáneo está integrado por muebles de madera y metal con un diseño depurado.

Una sala da pranzo in stile contemporaneo è integrata da mobili in legno e metallo, con un design depurato.

Uma sala de jantar de estilo contemporâneo é composta por móveis de madeira e metal com um design elegante.

En modern matsal består av trä- och metallmöbler i rena linjer.

BATHROOM
SALLE DE BAINS
BAD
BADKAMER
BAÑO
BAGNO
CASA DE BANHO
BADRUMMET

Built-in bathtubs make better use of space and benches and shelves can be incorporated in the same structure. It is important that the cladding does not filter water.

Les baignoires en maçonnerie optimisent l'espace, permettant de réunir dans la même structure des surfaces d'appoint et des étagères. Il est très important de choisir un revêtement étanche.

Eingebaute Badewannen nutzen den Platz besser aus und ermöglichen außerdem Bänke und Regale derselben Struktur anzubauen. Es ist sehr wichtig, darauf zu achten, dass die Beschichtung kein Wasser durchlässt.

Gemetselde badkuipen benutten de ruimte beter en maken het bovendien mogelijk om banken en planken daarnaast te creëren, alle in dezelfde structuur. Houd er bij de bekleding rekening mee dat het geen water doorlaat.

Las bañeras de obra aprovechan mejor el espacio y permiten además crear bancos y estantes adjuntos, todo en una misma estructura. Es muy importante tener en cuenta que el revestimiento no filtre el agua.

Le vasche da bagno in muratura sfruttano meglio lo spazio e consentono inoltre di creare panche e ripiani annessi, il tutto all'interno di una stessa struttura. È molto importante fare in modo che il rivestimento non lasci filtrare l'acqua.

As banheiras de alvenaria aproveitam melhor o espaço e permitem também criar bancos e estantes, tudo na mesma estrutura. É muito importante assegurar que o revestimento não permite a infiltração da água.

Med ett inbyggt badkar utnyttjar man utrymmet bättre och dessutom kan man skapa bänkar och hyllor i en och samma struktur. Det är mycket viktigt att se till att beläggningen inte släpper igenom vatten.

Fully integrate the bath by cladding it with the same material as the floor and the wall; this will visually enlarge the bath area.

Revêtir la baignoire avec le même matériau que le sol et le mur permet de l'intégrer complètement à l'ensemble et élargit visuellement la surface de la salle de bain.

Wenn Sie die Badewanne in derselben Weise wie den Boden und die Wand beschichten, passt alles zusammen, und das Bad wirkt größer.

Als u de badkuip op dezelfde wijze betegeld als de vloer en de muur, is die steen helemaal geïntegreerd en lijkt het gedeelte van de badkuip groter.

Si revistes la bañera de la misma manera que el suelo y la pared, aquella quedará plenamente integrada y ampliará visualmente el área del baño.

Se si riveste la vasca nello stesso modo del pavimento e della parete, questa sarà completamente integrata e amplierà visivamente la zona del bagno.

Se na banheira for aplicado o revestimento utilizado no solo e na parede, a mesma ficará plenamente integrada e ampliará visualmente a área da casa de banho.

Om du täcker badkaret med samma material som golvet och väggarna kommer det att vara helt integrerat och badrummet kommer att verka större.

Install a shower for personal cleanliness and an attached bath to enjoy long relaxing baths: the perfect combination that does not require too much space.

Une douche pour se laver et une baignoire pour profiter de longs bains relaxants : une combinaison parfaite qui ne demande pas trop d'espace.

Eine Dusche für die Körperpflege und daneben eine Badewanne, um lange "Ruhebäder zu genießen: eine perfekte Kombination, die nicht zu viel Platz verlangt.

Een douche voor lichaamsverzorging en een badkuip om te genieten van lang badderen: een perfecte combinatie die niet al te veel ruimte inneemt.

Ducha para el aseo y bañera adjunta para disfrutar de largos baños de relax: una combinación perfecta que no requiere demasiado espacio.

Doccia e vasca annessa per godere di lunghi bagni all'insegna del relax: una combinazione perfetta che non richiede spazio eccessivo.

O duche para a higiene diária em conjunto com a banheira para desfrutar de longos banhos relaxantes: uma combinação perfeita que não requer demasiado espaço.

En dusch för att sköta hygienen och ett intilligande bad för långa avslappnande bad: en perfekt kombination som inte kräver alltför mycket plats.

Use the wall cladding to differentiate and identify the bathtub area and the shower area.

Le revêtement du mur sert à différencier la partie occupée par la baignoire de celle où se trouve la douche.

Verwenden Sie verschiedene Wandverkleidungen, um die Bereiche von Badewanne und Dusche abzugrenzen.

Gebruik de betegeling van de muur om onderscheid te maken tussen de zone van de badkuip en de douche en deze te definiëren.

Usa el revestimiento de la pared para diferenciar y definir la zona de la bañera y la de la ducha.

Usa il rivestimento della parete per differenziare e definire la zona della vasca e quella della doccia.

Use o revestimento da parede para diferenciar e distinguir a zona da banheira e a do duche.

Använd väggbeläggningen för att skilja badet från duschutrymmet.

Install a shower in a transparent glass booth so as not to disrupt the generous amount of natural light.

Installer la douche dans une cabine en verre transparent permet à la lumière naturelle d'éclairer cette partie de la pièce.

Um den großzügigen natürlichen Lichteinfall nicht zu behindern, installieren Sie die Dusche in einer durchsichtigen Glaskabine.

Om de inval van daglicht niet te onderbreken kunt u de douche in een transparante glazen cabine installeren.

Para no interrumpir la generosa entrada de luz natural, instala la ducha dentro de una cabina de cristal transparente.

Per non interrompere il generoso ingresso di luce naturale, è preferibile inserire la doccia dentro una cabina di vetro trasparente.

Para não interromper uma entrada de luz natural generosa, instale o duche dentro de uma cabina de vidro transparente.

För att inte förhindra att dagsljuset släpps in kan man placera duschen i en genomskinlig kabin.

Opt for an open partition complete with a fixed glass
to let light into the bathtub.

Pour laisser passer la lumière jusqu'à la baignoire, vous
pouvez construire une cloison partiellement ouverte,
complétée d'une plaque de verre fixe.

Entscheiden Sie sich für eine offene Zwischenwand,
die durch ein fest eingebautes Glas ergänzt wird, um Licht
in die Badewanne zu lassen.

Kies voor een open tussenschot dat afgemaakt wordt
met een vast glas, zodat er licht tot de badkuip door kan
dringen.

Decántate por un tabique abierto que se completa
con un cristal fijo para dejar pasar la luz en la bañera.

Opta per un divisorio aperto, rifinito da un vetro fisso
per lasciare passare la luce nella zona doccia.

Opte por uma parede aberta que se completa com
um vidro fixo para deixar passar luz para a banheira.

Välj en öppen mellanvägg som kompletteras med en fast
glasskiva så att ljuset når badkaret.

If you want privacy when bathing, organize the shower space within a few low built-in walls.

Si vous tenez à votre intimité au moment de vous laver, vous pouvez organiser l'espace de la douche à l'intérieur de murets en maçonnerie.

Wenn Sie beim Baden Unabhängigkeit möchten, richten Sie den Duschbereich innerhalb von niedrigen Mauern ein.

Wilt u privacy tijdens het baden, richt de ruimte van de douche dan in tussen gemetselde muurtjes.

Si quieres independencia a la hora de bañarte, organiza el espacio de la ducha dentro de unos muretes de obra.

Se desideri fare della zona doccia uno spazio indipendente, definiscilo tramite pareti in muratura.

Caso pretenda privacidade na hora do banho, organize o espaço do duche dentro de umas paredes em alvenaria.

Om du vill duscha ostört kan du placera duschen innanför specialbyggda murar.

Choose a preferably smooth and light colored fabric for shower curtains so that they integrate into the environment. Fabrics with patterns and many colors are difficult to combine.

Les rideaux de la douche auront de préférence une couleur claire et unie pour mieux s'intégrer à l'environnement. En effet, il est difficile d'associer les textiles imprimés et très colorés.

Wählen Sie für die Duschvorhänge einen möglichst glatten, hellen Stoff, damit er sich in die Umgebung einfügt. Textilien mit Mustern und vielen Farben sind schwierig zu kombinieren.

Kies voor de douchegordijnen van bij voorkeur een effen stof, in een lichte kleur die in de ruimte integreert. Bedrukte en veelkleurige stoffen zijn lastig te combineren.

Elige para las cortinas de la ducha un tejido preferentemente liso y de color claro para que se integren en el ambiente. Los textiles con estampados y muchos colores son difíciles de combinar.

Per le tende della doccia, scegli un tessuto preferibilmente liscio e di colore chiaro, affinché si integrino con l'ambiente. I tessuti stampati e con molti colori sono difficili da combinare.

Escolha para as cortinas do duche um tecido de preferência liso e de cor clara para que se integre no ambiente. Os têxteis com estampados e muitas cores são difíceis de combinar.

Välj duschdraperi i ett enfärgat tyg i en ljus färg som passar miljön. Textilier med mönster och många färger är svåra att kombinera.

Ceramic tiling not only resists moisture and is long-lasting, but it is also available in a range of colors that can create high-contrasting modern bathrooms.

Le carrelage résiste non seulement à l'humidité et à l'usure mais il offre une gamme de couleurs permettant de créer des salles de bain modernes et très audacieuses.

Keramikbeschichtungen lassen keine Feuchtigkeit durch und verändern sich nicht durch Abnutzung. Zudem bieten sie eine große Farbauswahl und ermöglichen die Gestaltung von modernen, kontrastreichen Bädern.

Keramiek bekledingen zijn bestand tegen vocht en zijn slijtvast. Bovendien bieden zij een kleurengamma waarmee moderne badkamers met groot contrast kunnen worden ontworpen.

El revestimiento cerámico resiste la humedad y el desgaste, además de ofrecer una gama de colores que hacen posible crear baños modernos de alto contraste.

Il rivestimento ceramico resiste all'umidità e all'usura, oltre a offrire una gamma di colori che consente di creare bagni moderni e di grande contrasto.

O revestimento cerâmico resiste à humidade e ao desgaste para além de oferecer uma gama de cores que permite criar casas de banho modernas com grandes contrastes.

Beläggning av kakel är motståndskraftigt mot fukt och slitage. Dessutom finns det i ett stort färgutbud vilket gör att man kan skapa moderna badrum med stora kontraster.

Modern bathrooms normally have plain walls but you may add mosaic tiles to one wall generally the wall behind the vanity unit.

Les salles de bain modernes ont des revêtements unis, rehaussés – en général sur le mur du meuble du lavabo – par des dessins réalisés avec du carrelage en mosaïque.

Moderne Bäder haben glatte Wandbeschichtungen, aber man kann eine Wand - normalerweise die, an dem sich das Waschbecken befindet - mit Mosaikfliesen verkleiden.

Moderne badkamers hebben vlakke bekledingen, maar een wand (in het algemeen die waar het meubelstuk van de wastafel tegenaan staat) met in mozaïek gemaakte tekeningen is toegestaan.

Los baños modernos llevan revestimientos lisos pero admiten una pared –en general, la del mueble del lavabo– con dibujos realizados con mosaicos.

I bagni moderni hanno rivestimenti lisci ma consentono di avere una parete – solitamente quella del mobile del lavabo – decorata a mosaico.

As casas de banho modernas possuem revestimentos lisos mas é possível aplicar numa parede – geralmente a do móvel do lavatório – desenhos realizados com mosaicos.

Moderna badrum har enfärgade beläggningar men kan ha en vägg, oftast den där handfatet är placerat, med ett mönster i mosaik.

The contrast of polished concrete in wet areas with treated wood in the rest of the bathroom creates a modern and elegant ambience.

Le contraste entre le béton poli, utilisé dans la partie consacrée à l'eau et le bois traité, présent sur la surface restante, crée une atmosphère moderne et élégante.

Der Kontrast von poliertem Zement in der Nasszone mit dem behandelten Holz im Rest des Badezimmers bewirkt eine moderne und elegante Atmosphäre.

Het contrast van gepolijste cement in het watergedeelte met behandeld hout in de rest van de badkamer geeft een moderne en elegante sfeer.

El contraste del cemento pulido en la zona de aguas con la madera tratada en el resto del baño genera un ambiente moderno y elegante.

Il contrasto del cemento lucidato nella zona doccia/vasca con il legno trattato che riveste il resto del bagno genera un ambiente moderno ed elegante.

O contraste conseguido entre o cimento polido no espaço reservado ao banho e a madeira tratada no resto da casa de banho, cria um ambiente moderno e elegante.

Kontrasten med slipad cement i vattenområdet med behandlat trä i resten av badrummet skapar en modern och elegant miljö.

To withstand moisture in the bathroom, choose treated wood that is hard and non-porous with an oil finish that works as a thermal insulator.

Pour résister à l'humidité de la salle de bain, le bois choisi doit être traité, particulièrement dur, peu poreux et recouvert d'une couche d'huile qui l'isole thermiquement.

Für die Feuchtigkeitsresistenz des Bades wählen Sie besonders hartes, mit Öl behandeltes Holz, das wenig porös ist und als Wärmeisolierung dient.

Kies, om weerstand te bieden tegen de vochtigheid in de badkamer, voor behandeld, duurzaam en weinig poreus hout met afwerking in olie, voor een warmte-isolerende werking.

Para resistir la humedad del baño, elige madera tratada, especialmente dura, poco porosa y con un acabado de aceite que funcione a modo de aislante térmico.

Per resistere all'umidità del bagno, scegli un legno trattato, particolarmente duro, poco poroso e con una finitura all'olio che serva da isolante termico.

Para resistir à humidade do banho, opte por madeira tratada, especialmente sólida, pouco porosa e com um acabamento de óleo que funciona como um isolamento térmico.

Välj hårt, behandlat trä som står emot badrummets fukt och som är lite poröst och har lackerats med olja som fungerar som värmeisolering.

Synthetic parquet flooring has designs that resemble different types of wood. They are easily cleaned and withstand moisture.

Les sols en parquet synthétique ont des dessins imitant différents types de bois. Ils résistent à l'humidité et sont faciles à nettoyer.

Böden aus synthetischem Parkett haben ein Design, das den verschiedenen Holzarten ähnelt, und sie habenden großen Vorteil, dass sie feuchtigkeitsresistent und einfach zu reinigen sind.

Synthetische parketvloeren hebben een ontwerp dat lijkt op verschillende soorten hout en hebben het grote voordeel dat ze beter bestand zijn tegen vocht en gemakkelijk te reinigen zijn.

Los suelos de parqué sintético tienen diseños que se asemejan a diferentes tipos de madera y cuentan con la gran ventaja de resistir la humedad y ser fáciles de limpiar.

I pavimenti in parqué sintetico riproducono diverse tipologie di legno e hanno il grande vantaggio di resistere all'umidità ed essere facili da pulire.

Os pavimentos de parqué sintético têm padrões que se assemelham a diferentes tipos de madeira e possuem a grande vantagem de resistir à humidade e de permitirem uma limpeza fácil.

Golv av syntetisk parkett finns i utföranden som liknar olika trätyper och har fördelen att de står emot väta och är lätta att rengöra.

The new ceramic designs have finishes and patterns
identical to stone and are cheaper.

Les nouveaux motifs des carrelages ont des finitions
imitant la pierre et sont très bon marché.

Die neuen Keramik-Designs besitzen ähnliche Oberflächen
und Motive wie Naturstein und sind billiger.

Moderne ontwerpen van keramiek hebben afwerkingen en
motieven die identiek zijn aan steen en die goedkoper zijn.

Los nuevos diseños cerámicos presentan acabados y
motivos idénticos a la piedra y que resultan más baratos.

I nuovi prodotti ceramici presentano finiture e motivi
identici alla pietra, con un costo nettamente inferiore.

Os novos padrões cerâmicos apresentam acabamentos
e motivos idênticos à pedra e tornam-se mais baratos.

Nya keramiktyper har utföranden och motiv som
är identiskt lika sten men billigare.

Replace the traditional vanity unit with a free-standing sink, supported on a built-in or wooden unit.

Le lavabo traditionnel peut être remplacé par un élément plus original, posé sur un meuble en maçonnerie ou en bois.

Ersetzen Sie das traditionelle Waschbecken durch ein freistehendes Handwaschbecken auf einem eingebauten Unterschrank oder einem aus Holz.

Vervang een traditionele wastafel door een los exemplaar dat op een gemetseld of houten meubelstuk staat.

Sustituye el lavabo tradicional por un lavamanos exento, apoyado sobre un mueble de obra o de madera.

Sostituisci il lavabo tradizionale con un lavamano spoglio, appoggiato su un mobile in muratura o in legno.

Substitua o lavatório tradicional por um lavatório independente, apoiado sobre um móvel de alvenaria ou de madeira.

Ersätt det traditionella handfatet med ett fristående tvättfat, placerat ovanpå en specialbyggd möbel i murverk eller trä.

Opt for washbasin proportional to the available area on the vanity unit and leave a space of at least 8 inches on each side so that water does not splash.

Le lavabo doit avoir une dimension proportionnelle à la surface disponible du meuble. Il faut laisser au moins 20 cm de chaque côté pour éviter les éclaboussures.

Entscheiden Sie sich für ein Waschbecken, das der verfügbaren Fläche der Waschtischplatte proportional ist, und lassen Sie an beiden Seiten mindestens 20 cm Platz übrig, damit das Wasser nicht spritzt.

Kies een wastafel waarvan de afmeting proportioneel is met de beschikbare oppervlakte van het werkblad en laat aan weerszijden een ruimte van tenminste 20 cm over, tegen opspattend water.

Decántate por un lavabo de tamaño proporcional a la superficie disponible en la encimera y deja un espacio de al menos 20 cm de cada lado para que no salpique el agua.

Opta per un lavabo di dimensioni proporzionali alla superficie disponibile sul ripiano e lascia uno spazio di almeno 20 cm su ciascun lato per evitare la fuoriuscita di acqua.

Escolha um lavatório de tamanho proporcional à superfície disponível na bancada e deixe um espaço de pelo menos 20 cm de cada lado para que a água não salpique.

Välj ett handfat i en storlek som passar den tillgängliga ytan i arbetsbänken och lämna minst 20 cm på varje sidan för att inte vattnet ska stänka.

The cantilever vanity unit visually lightens this part of the bathroom, in particular when installing two washbasins.

Une étagère murale allège visuellement cette zone de la salle de bain, en particulier si on y installe deux lavabos.

Die freischwebende Waschtischplatte lässt diesen Bereich des Bades leichter wirken, besonders dann, wenn man zwei Waschbecken installiert.

Het vooruitstekende werkblad maakt dit deel van de badkamer optisch lichter, vooral als er twee wastafels worden geïnstalleerd.

La encimera en volado aligera visualmente este sector del baño, especialmente cuando se instalan dos lavamanos.

Il ripiano sospeso alleggerisce visivamente questo settore del bagno, soprattutto quando si inseriscono due lavelli.

A bancada em suspensão torna visualmente mais leve esta zona da casa de banho, especialmente quando são instalados dois lavatórios.

En svängd skiva gör utrymmet visuellt lättare, speciellt om man installerar två handfat.

Make the most of space with a fitted wardrobe underneath the vanity unit including drawers and open shelves.

Un placard sur mesure sous le lavabo avec des tiroirs et des étagères ouvertes permet d'optimiser l'espace.

Nutzen Sie den Platz mit einem maßgefertigten Schrank unter der Waschtischplatte, der Schubladen und offene Fächer enthält, maximal aus.

Benut de ruimte optimaal met een op maat gemaakte kast onder het werkblad, met daarin laden en open planken.

Aprovecha al máximo el espacio con un armario hecho a medida debajo de la encimera que incluya cajones y estantes abiertos.

Sfrutta al massimo lo spazio con un armadio su misura sotto il ripiano, comprendente cassetti e ripiani e aperti.

Aproveite ao máximo o espaço com um armário feito à medida sob a bancada que inclua gavetas e estantes abertas.

Utnyttja utrymmet maximalt med ett specialbyggt skåp under ytan som innehåller lådor och öppna hyllor.

Install two sturdy wooden shelves: one as a vanity unit to support the washbasin and another as a shelf. Boxes are a great way to keep the objects organized out of sight.

Vous pouvez installer deux planches en bois résistant servant respectivement de plan d'appui pour le lavabo et d'étagère. Les boîtes sont une excellente solution pour ranger les objets.

Installieren Sie zwei Regalbretter aus widerstandsfähigem Holz: Eins als Waschtischplatte für die Waschbecken und das andere als Regal. Schachteln sind eine exzellente Lösung, um Gegenstände geordnet außer Sichtweite zu halten.

Monteer twee resistente houten planken: een die dienst doet als werkblad om de wastafel op te zetten en een als plank. Dozen zijn een uitstekende manier om voorwerpen netjes en buiten het zicht te bewaren.

Instala dos baldas de madera resistente: una a modo de encimera para apoyar el lavamanos y otra como estante. Las cajas son una excelente solución para mantener los objetos ordenados fuera de la vista.

Installa due mensole di legno resistente: una servirà da ripiano per appoggiare il lavello e un'altra da mensola. Le scatole sono una soluzione eccellente per mantenere in ordine e nascondere gli oggetti.

Instale duas prateleiras de madeira resistente: uma como bancada de apoio ao lavatório e outra como estante. As caixas são uma excelente solução para manter os objectos ordenados fora da vista.

Instellera två hyllor av slitstarkt trä: en som en slags skiva som stödjer handfatet och den andra som hylla. Lådor är ett utmärkt sätt att ha alla föremål ordnade och utom synhåll.

Place a bench with a shelf underneath the vanity top to store extra towels or a box with items such as the hair dryer, creams, extra toilet paper, etc.

Vous pouvez placer un tabouret avec étagère sous le plan du lavabo pour y ranger les serviettes ou des boîtes contenant des objets tels le sèche-cheveux, les crèmes, la réserve de papier toilette, etc.

Stellen Sie eine Bank mit einem Regalfach unter die Waschtischplatte des Waschbeckens, um Handtücher oder eine Schachtel mit Gegenständen wie Föhn, Cremes, Toilettenpapierreserve, usw. unterzubringen.

Zet een bankje met een plank onder het werkblad van de wastafel, om schone handdoeken op te leggen, of een doos om voorwerpen zoals de föhn, crèmes, of toiletpapier in op te bergen.

Sitúa un banco con estante debajo de la encimera del lavamanos para colocar las toallas de repuesto o una caja con objetos como el secador, las cremas, la reserva de papel higiénico, etc.

Posiziona una panca con pianetto sotto il ripiano del lavandino per sistemarvi asciugamani di riserva o una scatola dove riporre asciugacapelli, creme, carta igienica, ecc.

Coloque um banco com prateleira por baixo da bancada do lavatório onde possa arrumar as toalhas limpas ou uma caixa com objectos como o secador, os cremes, a reserva de papel higiénico, etc.

Placera en bänk med en hylla under skivan med handfatet där du kan placera extra handdukar eller en låda för saker som hårtork, krämer, extra toalettpapper etc.

The fluid and dynamic forms of the washbasin design makes them striking decorative objects in the bathroom.

Les formes fluides et dynamiques des lavabos design en font des objets de décoration qui enrichissent la salle de bain.

Die fließenden und dynamischen Formen der Designer-Waschbecken verwandeln diese in dekorative Objekte, die das Bad zu etwas Besonderem machen.

Design wastafels met vloeiende en dynamische vormen maken deze tot decoratieve voorwerpen die de badkamer accentueren.

Las formas fluidas y dinámicas de los lavamanos de diseño los convierten en objetos decorativos que jerarquizan el baño.

Le forme fluide e dinamiche dei lavandini di design ne fanno oggetti decorativi che danno enfasi all'ambiente bagno.

As formas fluidas e dinâmicas dos lavatórios design convertem-nos em objectos decorativos que dominam a casa de banho.

Flödande och dynamiska former på handfatet gör det till ett dekorativt föremål som är i badrummets blickfång.

There are many different ways to display the toilet paper beyond the traditional cylinder attached to the wall. Opt for boxes and floor stands that are easier to adapt to the space.

Outre le traditionnel cylindre collé au mur, il existe de nombreuses façons de poser le papier toilette : les boîtes et les supports sur pied s'adaptent plus facilement à l'espace.

Außer dem traditionellen an der Wand befestigten Rollen gibt es viele Möglichkeiten, das Toilettenpapier anzubringen. Entscheiden Sie sich für Kästen und Ständer, die sich leichter an den Raum anpassen.

Naast cilindervormige toiletrolhouders zijn veel andere manieren om het toiletpapier te bewaren. Kies bijvoorbeeld voor dozen en staanders die eenvoudiger kunnen worden aangepast aan de ruimte.

Existen muchas maneras de colocar el papel higiénico más allá del tradicional cilindro adosado a la pared. Decántate por cajas y soportes de pie que se adapten fácilmente al espacio.

Vi sono molti modi di sistemare la carta igienica, oltre al tradizionale cilindro fissato alla parete. Opta per scatole e supporti, più facilmente adattabili allo spazio a disposizione.

Existem muitas maneiras de tornar o papel higiénico algo mais do que o tradicional cilindro fixo à parede. Escolha caixas e suportes verticais que são mais fáceis de adaptar ao espaço.

Det finns många sätt att placera toalettpapper förutom den traditionella vägghållaren. Istället kan du välja en låda eller en golvställning som kan anpassas till utrymmet.

Separating the toilet with a sliding door or stone wall
is practical for homes with one bathroom.

Séparer les sanitaires du reste de la salle de bain par
une porte coulissante ou un mur en maçonnerie est une
solution très pratique.

Die Trennung der Sanitärzone durch eine Schiebetür oder
niedrige Mauer ist sehr praktisch für Wohnungen mit nur
einem Bad.

De afscheiding van het toiletgedeelte door een schuifdeur
of gemetselde muur is heel praktisch voor huizen met
slechts een badkamer.

La separación de la zona de sanitarios mediante una
puerta corredera o murete de obra resulta muy práctica
para casas con un solo baño.

La separazione della zona dei sanitari tramite una porta
scorrevole o una parete in muratura è molto pratica nelle
case che dispongono di un solo bagno.

A separação da zona sanitária através de uma porta
de correr ou de uma parede de alvenaria torna-se uma
solução muito prática para casas com apenas uma casa
de banho.

Att skilja av toalettdelen med en skjutdörr eller en låg mur
är mycket praktiskt i hem med bara ett badrum.

If the shower and the toilets are installed on the same wall, maximize space with a partition to separate them and a door to give them independence.

Si la douche et les sanitaires sont installés sur le même mur, vous pouvez optimiser l'espace avec un muret qui le sépare et une porte qui les rend indépendants.

Wenn die Dusche und die Toilette an derselben Wand installiert sind, optimieren Sie den Platz mit einer Zwischenwand, um diese Bereiche zu trennen und einer Tür, um sie voneinander unabhängig zu machen.

Als de douche en het toilet tegen een muur zijn geïnstalleerd, optimaliseer de ruimte dan met een tussenschot om deze van elkaar te scheiden en een deur voor onafhankelijke ruimtes.

Si la ducha y los sanitarios están instalados sobre una misma pared, optimiza el espacio con un tabique para separarlos y una puerta para darles independencia.

Se la doccia e i sanitari sono appoggiati su una stessa parete, ottimizza lo spazio con un divisorio per separarli e inserisci una porta per rendere i vari spazi indipendenti tra loro.

Se o duche e a zona sanitária estiverem instalados sobre uma mesma parede, optimize o espaço com uma divisória para separar as zonas e uma porta para permitir privacidade.

Om duschen och toaletten är placerade på samma vägg kan man optimera utrymmet genom en mellanvägg som skiljer dem åt och en dörr för avskildhet.

Convert your bathroom into a spa and place the bathtub at ground level to create breadth.

Votre salle de bain peut avoir l'allure d'un spa : la baignoire à même le sol permet de gagner de l'espace.

Sorgen Sie dafür, dass Ihr Bad einem *spa* ähnelt und lassen Sie die Badewanne in den Boden ein, um Geräumigkeit zu gewinnen.

Geef uw badkamer het uiterlijk van een *spa* en laat de badkuip in de vloer leggen om ruimte te besparen.

Haz que tu baño se asemeje a un *spa* y sitúa la bañera a nivel del suelo para ganar amplitud.

Trasforma il tuo bagno in una piccola *spa* e sistema la vasca al livello del pavimento per guadagnare ampiezza.

Faça com que a sua casa de banho se assemelhe a um *spa* e coloque a banheira ao nível do solo para ganhar amplitude.

Förvandla ditt badrum till ett spa och placera badkaret i golvhöjd för att få större utrymme.

Leave a blank strip above the tiles so that the wall seems higher.

Le mur paraît plus haut si on laisse une bande blanche au-dessus du carrelage.

Lassen Sie einen weißen Streifen über der gefliesten Fläche frei, damit die Wand höher wirkt.

Laat boven de zone met tegeltjes een strook wit open, zodat de muur hoger lijkt.

Deja una franja en blanco por encima de la zona de azulejos para que la pared parezca más alta.

Lascia una fascia bianca sopra la zona mattonellata affinché la parete sembri più alta.

Deixe uma faixa em branco por cima da zona de azulejos para que a parede pareça mais alta.

Lämna ett vitt parti ovanför kaklet, det gör att väggen verkar längre.

Use the bathroom to store accessories such as hats and pendants, and convert this space into a dressing room.

Vous pouvez utiliser la salle de bain pour ranger des accessoires tels les chapeaux et les pendentifs, comme sur une coiffeuse.

Nutzen Sie das Bad, um Accessoires wie Hüte und Anhänger aufzubewahren und gewinnen Sie wieder die Funktion dieses Raumes als Boudoir.

Gebruik de badkamer om accessoires zoals hoeden en hangers te bewaren, en herstel in deze ruimte het concept van toilettafel in ere.

Utiliza el baño para guardar accesorios como sombreros y colgantes, y recuperar el concepto de este espacio como tocador.

Utilizza il bagno per riporre accessori come cappelli e collane e recupera l'idea di uno spazio dedicato alla toeletta.

Utilize a casa de banho para guardar acessórios como chapéus e colares, recupere o conceito deste espaço como toucador.

Använd badrummet för att förvara accessoarer som hattar och halsband. Använd badrummet som påklädningsrum.

To create a warm ambience, decorate with paintings and photo frames of materials and colors in the same range as the mirror.

Pour créer une atmosphère chaude, vous pouvez décorer la pièce avec des tableaux et des porte-photos conçus dans des matériaux et des couleurs de la même gamme que le miroir.

Um eine warme Atmosphäre zu schaffen, dekorieren Sie den Spiegel mit Bildern und Fotorahmen aus Materialien und Farben im gleichen Stil.

Voor een warme sfeer kunt u decoreren met schilderijen en fotolijsten van materialen en kleuren in hetzelfde gamma als de spiegel.

Para crear un ambiente cálido, decora con cuadros y portarretratos de materiales y colores de la misma gama del espejo.

Per creare un ambiente accogliente, aggiungi quadri e portaritratti in materiali e colori della stessa gamma dello specchio.

Para criar um ambiente quente, decore com quadros e porta-retratos de materiais e cores do mesmo tipo que o espelho.

För att skapa en varm atmosfär kan du inreda med tavlor och ramar i samma material och färgnyanser som spegeln.

An easy way to counteract the coldness of this microcement finish is to display decorative details in warm materials such as natural fiber and wood.

Une manière facile pour mitiger la froideur transmise par le revêtement en microciment consiste à ajouter des détails décoratifs conçus avec des matériaux chauds comme la fibre naturelle et le bois.

Eine einfache Art, der Kälte, die die Mikrozement-Flächen ausstrahlen entgegenzuwirken besteht darin, dekorative Objekte aus warmen Materialien wie Naturfaser und Holz aufzustellen.

Een eenvoudige manier om de koude sfeer die de afwerking in microcement uitademt te neutraliseren is om decoratieve details van warme materialen zoals natuurvezel en hout neer te zetten.

Una manera fácil de contrarrestar la frialdad que transmite el acabado de microcemento es colocar detalles decorativos de materiales cálidos como la fibra natural y la madera.

Un modo facile di contrastare la freddezza che trasmette la finitura in microcemento è sistemare dettagli decorativi in materiali caldi, come le fibre naturali e il legno.

Uma maneira fácil de neutralizar a frieza transmitida pelo acabamento em microcimento consiste em utilizar pormenores decorativos de materiais quentes como a fibra natural e a madeira.

Ett enkelt sätt att motarbeta den kyla som mikrocementbeläggningen utstrålar är att placera ut dekorativa föremål i varma material som naturfiber och trä.

Towels in one color add to the elegance of the bathroom. Try and use the same color for the rest of textiles, such as the mat or shower curtain.

Les serviettes d'une couleur unies rendent la salle de bain plus élégante. Si le reste des textiles – le tapis de bain ou les rideaux de la douche - sont dans la même tonalité, l'effet est renforcé.

Einfarbige Handtücher tragen dazu bei, das Bad eleganter zu machen. Umso mehr, wenn die anderen Textilien wie die Fußmatte oder der Duschvorhang vom selben Farbton sind.

Handdoeken in dezelfde kleur geven de badkamer iets elegants. Het is nog beter als ook de rest van de textiel, zoals het matje of het douchegordijn dezelfde tint hebben.

Las toallas de un solo color contribuyen a hacer más elegante el baño. Mejor aún si el resto de los textiles, como la alfombrilla o la cortina del baño, son del mismo tono.

Gli asciugamani monocolore contribuiscono a rendere il bagno più elegante. Meglio ancora se il resto dei tessuti, come il tappetino o la tenda del bagno, riprendono lo stesso tono.

As toalhas de uma só cor ajudam a tornar a casa de banho mais elegante. Melhor será ainda se os restantes elementos, como o tapete ou a cortina do duche, forem do mesmo tom.

Att alla handdukar är i samma färg gör badrummet mer elegant. Det är ännu bättre om resten av textilierna, som badrumsmattan och duschdraperiet är i samma nyans.

Make small bathrooms stand out with small decorative details that do not take up space such as a panel to support and frame the mirror.

Vous pouvez enrichir les salles de bain très petites avec des détails de décoration qui ne prennent pas de place, comme un panneau servant à suspendre et encadrer le miroir.

Werten Sie sehr kleine Bäder mit dekorativen Details auf, die keinen Platz wegnehmen, wie ein Paneel, das den Spiegel hält und einrahmt.

Gebruik in hele kleine badkamers decoratieve details die niet veel ruimte innemen, zoals een paneel dat dienst doet om de spiegel te ondersteunen en in te lijsten.

Jerarquiza los baños muy pequeños con detalles decorativos que no ocupen espacio, como un panel que sirva para sostener y enmarcar el espejo.

Dai enfasi ai bagni molto piccoli con dettagli decorativi che non occupino spazio, come un pannello che serve per sostenere e incorniciare lo specchio.

Confira personalidade às casas de banho muito pequenas com detalhes decorativos que não ocupem espaço, como um painel que sirva para sustentar e emoldurar o espelho.

Gör ett litet badrum mer attraktivt med dekorativa detaljer som inte tar mycket plats, som en panel som stödjer och ramar in spegeln.

OUTDOORS

L'EXTÉRIEUR

IM FREIEN

IN DE BUITENLUCHT

AL AIRE LIBRE

L'AMBIENTE ESTERNO

AO AR LIVRE

UTOMHUS

Hanging hammocks are ideal for relaxation for adults and for children to play with. If you do not have trees to tie them to use a column or fix a hook to the wall.

Les hamacs suspendus sont une excellente solution pour le repos des adultes et les jeux des enfants. Si vous n'avez pas d'arbres pour les accrocher, vous pouvez utiliser une colonne ou fixer un crochet au mur.

Hängematten sind ideal zum Ausruhen für Erwachsene und zum Spielen für die Kinder. Wenn Sie keine Bäume haben, um sie daran zu befestigen, benutzen Sie eine Säule oder schlagen Sie einen Haken in die Wand.

Hangmatten zijn ideaal voor volwassenen om te relaxen en voor kinderen om te spelen. Heeft u geen bomen om deze op te hangen, gebruik dan een zuil of hang ze aan een haak in de muur.

Las hamacas colgantes son ideales para el relax en el caso de los adultos y para el juego de los niños. Si no tienes árboles donde atarlas usa una columna o coloca un gancho en la pared.

Le amache sospese sono ideali per i momenti di relax, sia per gli adulti che per il gioco dei più piccoli. Se non disponi di alberi, usa una colonna o sistema un gancio su una parete.

As camas de rede são ideais para descontrair no caso dos adultos e para a brincadeira no caso das crianças. Caso não tenha árvores onde atar a cama de rede use um pilar ou aplique um gancho na parede.

En hängmatta är idealisk för vuxna att vila i och för barn att leka i. Om du inte har några träd där du kan hänga den kan du använda en pelare eller en krok i väggen.

Incorporate the living room into the garden through sliding doors blurring the boundaries of the living room, and use the same flooring on the interior and exterior.

Les portes coulissantes permettent d'intégrer le salon au jardin : ouvertes, elles effacent les limites de la pièce, grâce aussi au choix du même revêtement de sol à l'intérieur et à l'extérieur.

Verbinden Sie das Wohnzimmer mit dem Garten durch denselben Bodenbelag draußen wie drinnen und durch Schiebetüren, die, wenn sie geöffnet sind, die Grenzen des Zimmers verwischen.

Integreer de zitkamer met de tuin door middel van schuifdeuren die, als ze worden geopend, de grenzen van de kamer vervagen en door buiten en binnen dezelfde vloertegels te gebruiken.

Integra el salón en el jardín mediante puertas correderas que al abrirse desdibujan los límites de la habitación, y con el uso del mismo pavimento en el exterior que en el interior.

Unisci il salotto al giardino tramite delle porte scorrevoli che aprendosi ampliano i limiti della stanza, grazie anche all'uso dello stesso pavimento all'interno e all'esterno.

Integre a sala no jardim através de portas de correr que ao abrir retirem a delimitação do espaço. Para o efeito, use no exterior o mesmo pavimento usado no interior.

Bind samman vardagsrummet med trädgården genom skjutdörrar som gör gränsen mellan de två rummen mindre tydlig. Man kan också använda samma stengolv utomshus som inomhus.

Wood is one of the materials best suited to all styles of outdoor furniture in particular when they are located under a porch protected from the rain.

Le bois est l'un des matériaux qui s'adaptent le mieux à tous les styles d'extérieurs, surtout lorsque les meubles sont sous un porche qui les protège de la pluie.

Holz ist eins der Materialien, das sich am besten an alle Stilarten im Freien anpasst, vor allem, wenn sich die Möbel unter einem Verandadach befinden, das sie vor Regen schützt.

Hout is een van de materialen die zich het beste aanpassen aan alle stijlen voor buiten, met name als de meubels onder een overkapping worden gezet waar ze beschermd zijn tegen de regen.

La madera es uno de los materiales que mejor se adaptan a todos los estilos de exteriores, sobre todo cuando los muebles están debajo de un porche que los resguarda de la lluvia.

Il legno è uno dei materiali che meglio si adattano a tutti i tipi di ambienti esterni, soprattutto quando i mobili sono sotto un porticato che li protegge dalla pioggia.

A madeira é um dos materiais que melhor se adapta a todos os estilos de exteriores, sobretudo quando os móveis estão sob um alpendre que os protege da chuva.

Trä är ett av de material som bäst anpassar sig till olika utomhusmiljöer, speciellt när möblerna står under ett tak som skyddar dem mot regn.

Add a touch of green to the balcony with a continuous row of shrubs planted in a planter of the same material as the flooring.

Vous pouvez ajouter une touche verte à votre balcon avec une rangée ininterrompue d'arbustes plantés dans un bac fait dans le même matériau que le sol.

Begrünen Sie den Balkon mit einer ununterbrochenen Reihe von Büschen in einem Blumenkasten aus demselben Material, aus dem der Boden besteht.

Geef het balkon een groen accent met een ononderbroken rij struiken in een plantenbak van hetzelfde materiaal als de vloer.

Incluye un toque de verde en el balcón con una fila ininterrumpida de arbustos plantada en una jardinera del mismo material que el suelo.

Aggiungi un tocco di verde al balcone con una fila ininterrotta di piccoli cespugli piantati in un vascone dello stesso materiale del pavimento.

Inclua um toque de verde na varanda com uma fila contínua de arbustos plantada numa floreira feita do mesmo material que o pavimento.

Lägg till ett grönt inslag på balkongen med en hel häck av buskar som planteras i en låda i samma material som golvet.

Use plants and shrubs that reach a height of about three feet to define the garden space, thus maintaining privacy without losing the overview.

Utiliser des plantes et des arbustes atteignant environ un mètre de hauteur pour délimiter l'espace du jardin permet de préserver son intimité sans renoncer à la vue générale.

Verwenden Sie Pflanzen und Büsche, die ungefähr einen Meter hoch werden, um den Garten zu begrenzen. So erhalten Sie die Privatsphäre ohne die Aussicht zu verlieren.

Gebruik planten en struiken die ongeveer een meter hoog worden om de tuin af te bakenen, zodat uw privacy behouden blijft zonder dat het uitzicht belemmerd wordt.

Utiliza plantas y arbustos que alcancen una altura de aproximadamente un metro para delimitar el espacio del jardín, manteniendo así la privacidad sin perder la vista general.

Utilizza piante e arbusti che raggiungano un'altezza di circa un metro per delimitare lo spazio del giardino, mantenendo così la privacy senza perdere la vista generale.

Utilize plantas e arbustos que atinjam uma altura de aproximadamente um metro para delimitar o espaço do jardim, mantendo assim a privacidade sem perder a vista geral.

Använd växter och buskar som är ungefär en meter höga för att skärma av trädgårdens plats. Så får man mer avskildhet utan att förlora utsikt

To create a small outdoor dining area you only need a table and two chairs. If they are lightweight, you can change their position whenever you want.

Pour créer une petite salle à manger en plein air, il suffit d'une table et de quelques chaises. Si elles sont faciles à transporter, vous pouvez changer leur emplacement dans le jardin.

Um ein kleines Esszimmer im Freien zu schaffen, sind nur ein Tisch und zwei Stühle nötig. Sie sind leicht zu transportieren und man kann sie an verschiedenen Orten des Gartens aufstellen.

Voor een kleine eethoek buiten heeft u alleen maar een tafel en een paar stoelen nodig. Als ze gemakkelijk verplaatsbaar zijn kunnen ze binnen de tuin worden verplaatst tegen een andere achtergrond.

Para crear un pequeño comedor al aire libre solo son necesarias una mesa y un par de sillas. Si son fáciles de transportar puedes ir cambiándolas de escenario dentro del jardín.

Per creare una piccola sala da pranzo all'aperto bastano un tavolo e un paio di sedie. Se sono facili da trasportare, puoi di volta in volta cambiarne l'ubicazione all'interno del giardino.

Para criar um pequeno espaço de refeições ao ar livre são necessárias apenas uma mesa e um par de cadeiras. Se forem fáceis de transportar poderá mudá-las de lugar dentro do jardim.

För att skapa en mindre matplats utomhus behöver du bara ett bord och ett par stolar. Om de är lätta att förflytta kan du flytta dem till olika platser runt om i trädgården.

Take advantage of large trees to place a dining area under their crown. It's the best way to shelter from the sun.

Vous pouvez installer une salle à manger sous les grands arbres du jardin. C'est la meilleure façon pour se protéger du soleil.

Nutzen Sie die großen Bäume des Hauses aus, um einen Essplatz unter ihrer Krone einzurichten. Dies ist die beste Art, sich vor der Sonne zu schützen.

Gebruik grote bomen in de tuin om er een eethoek neer te zetten. Dat is de beste manier om uit de zon te zitten.

Aprovecha los árboles grandes de la casa para instalar un comedor debajo de su copa. Es la mejor manera de mantenerse al resguardo del sol.

Sfrutta gli alberi grandi del giardino per sistemare sotto la loro chioma un tavolo da pranzo. È il modo migliore per ripararsi dal sole.

Aproveite as árvores grandes da casa para instalar um espaço de refeições debaixo da respectiva copa. É a melhor forma de se manter protegido do sol.

Utnyttja trädgårdens stora träd för att placera en matplats under dess krona. Det är det bästa sättet att skydda sig mot solen.

Light the interior of the pool to prevent accidents at night, it means that it can be used at any time and emphasizes the design.

Éclairer l'intérieur de la piscine permet d'éviter les incidents nocturnes, de l'utiliser à n'importe quel moment de la journée et de mettre en valeur sa forme.

Beleuchten Sie das Schwimmbecken von innen, um Unfälle in der Nacht zu vermeiden. Die Innenbeleuchtung ermöglicht zudem die Benutzung des Beckens zu jeder Zeit und hebt sein Design hervor.

Verlicht het zwembad van binnen om 's avonds ongelukken te voorkomen. Zo kan het zwembad op ieder willekeurig tijdstip gebruikt worden en komt het ontwerp beter tot zijn recht.

Ilumina el interior de la piscina para evitar accidentes durante la noche, permitir su uso a cualquier hora y enfatizar el diseño.

Illumina l'interno della piscina per evitare incidenti durante la notte, poterla utilizzare in qualsiasi momento e dare enfasi al design della struttura.

Ilumine o interior da piscina para evitar acidentes durante a noite. Deste modo irá permitir a sua utilização a qualquer hora e realçar o design.

Ljussätt poolens interiör för att undvika olyckor på kvällen, så att man kan använda den när som helst och dessutom understryka dess design.

The furniture and facilities around the pool should be consistent in the shapes and materials to integrate the entire environment.

Les meubles et les installations autour de la piscine doivent respecter la cohérence des formes et des matériaux pour s'harmoniser avec l'environnement.

Die Möbel und Installationen rund um das Schwimmbecken sollten in Form und Material einheitlich sein, damit alles zu der Umgebung passt

Meubels en voorzieningen rond het zwembad moeten qua vorm en materiaal overeenkomen, zodat de ruimte een eenheid vormt.

Los muebles e instalaciones alrededor de la piscina deben guardar coherencia en las formas y materiales para integrar todo el ambiente.

I mobili e gli arredi intorno alla piscina devono essere coerenti con le forme e i materiali per integrarsi nell'ambiente.

Os móveis e instalações em redor da piscina devem manter a coerência nas formas e materiais utilizados de forma a integrarem-se no ambiente.

Möblerna och redskapen runt poolen bör vara av liknande former och material så att miljön blir enhetlig.

Anthracite and aluminum are the main materials used for new outdoor dining table sets resistant to all kinds of weather.

L'aluminium et le tissu en anthracite sont les stars du nouveau mobilier pour salle à manger d'extérieur, résistant à toutes les intempéries.

Aluminium und Anthrazitstoffe, die gegen alle Unbilden des Wetters resistent sind, spielen die Hauptrolle bei den neuen Esszimmermöbeln für draußen.

Aluminium en antraciet materialen zijn toonaangevend voor de nieuwe tuinmeubelensets en zijn bestand tegen allerlei weersomstandigheden.

Aluminio y tejido de antracita son los protagonistas de los nuevos juegos de comedor exterior resistentes a todas las inclemencias del tiempo.

Alluminio e tessuto antracite sono i protagonisti dei nuovi set da pranzo per esterni, resistenti a qualsiasi tipo di condizione metereologica.

O alumínio e o tecido de antracite são os elementos marcantes dos novos conjuntos para espaços de refeição ao ar livre, resistentes a todo tipo de inclemências do tempo.

Aluminium och antracitväv är viktiga inslag i de nya möblerna för utomhusbruk som står emot vädrets växlingar.

Furnish the exterior as if it were interior. Opt for highly durable materials and do not skimp on details such as decorative candles, textiles, carpets and curtains.

La décoration extérieure exige la même attention que l'intérieur. Il faut choisir des matériaux très résistants et ne pas lésiner sur les accessoires décoratifs comme les bougies, les tapis et les rideaux.

Statten Sie die Außenbereiche wie das Innere des Hauses aus, Verwenden Sie widerstandsfähige Materialien und sparen Sie nicht an dekorativen Einzelheiten wie Kerzen, Textilien, Teppichen und Vorhängen.

Richt de buitenruimte net zo in als een interieur. Kies voor degelijke materialen en beknibbel niet op decoratieve details zoals kaarsen, textiel, kleden en gordijnen.

Equipa el exterior como si fuese el interior. Recurre a materiales de alta resistencia y no escatimes en detalles decorativos como velas, textiles, alfombras y cortinas.

Arreda l'ambiente esterno come faresti con una stanza della casa. Ricorri a materiali altamente resistenti e non rinunciare a dettagli decorativi come candele, tessuti, tappeti e tende.

Equipe o exterior como se fosse o interior. Escolha materiais de elevada resistência e não poupe em pormenores decorativos como velas, têxteis, tapetes e cortinas.

Utrusta trädgården som om den vore husets interiör. Använd material med hög hållbarhet och spara inte in på dekorativa detaljer som ljus, textilier, mattor och gardiner.

The blinds of a semi-translucent fabric around the porch control the heat and air currents. Raw or very clear colors are best so as not to create a sense of closure.

Réalisés dans un textile semi-translucide, les stores entourant le porche règlent l'entrée de la chaleur et les courants d'air. Les couleurs claires et l'écru sont à préférer car ils ne provoquent pas la sensation d'enfermement.

Die Stores aus einem halbtransparenten Stoff um die Veranda herum regulieren Wärme und Luftzug. Es ist besser, wenn sie naturfarben oder sehr hell sind, damit sie kein Gefühl von Eingeschlossensein erwecken.

Door rolgordijnen van een halfdoorschijnende stof rond de veranda op te hangen, kunnen de warmte en luchtstromen worden gecontroleerd. Deze hebben bij voorkeur naturel of hele lichte kleuren, zodat ze niet het gevoel geven ingesloten te zijn.

Los estores de un textil semitranslúcido alrededor del porche controlan la entrada del calor y las corrientes de aire. Mejor que sean de colores crudos o muy claros para que no generen sensación de encierro.

Le veneziane in tessuto traslucido intorno al porticato consentono di gestire l'ingresso del calore e delle correnti d'aria. È meglio optare per colori crema o comunque molto chiari per evitare la sensazione di chiusura.

Os estores em têxtil semitranslúcido em redor do alpendre controlam a entrada do calor e as correntes de ar. Será melhor que sejam de cores cruas ou muito claras para que não criem a sensação de confinamento.

Gardiner av ett halvgenomskinligt tyg runt uteplatsen skyddar den mot hetta och luftströmmar. De bör helst vara i neutrala eller ljusa färger så att det inte känns instängt.

Candles create a special atmosphere outdoors. Place them alone or lanterns, on steps, on the edge of the balcony or in the corners of the courtyard.

À l'extérieur, les bougies créent une atmosphère spéciale, que vous les placiez toute seules ou dans une lanterne, sur les marches des escaliers, sur la bordure du balcon ou aux coins de la cour.

Kerzen schaffen im Freien eine besondere Atmosphäre. Stellen Sie sie alleine oder innerhalb von Laternen auf, auf Treppenstufen, am Rand des Balkons oder in den Ecken des Patios.

Kaarsen brengen een speciale sfeer buiten. Plaats ze los of in lantaarns op de treden van de trap, aan de rand van het balkon of in de hoeken van de patio.

Las velas crean un ambiente especial en el exterior. Colócalas, solas o dentro de faroles, en los peldaños de las escaleras, en el borde del balcón o en las esquinas del patio.

Le candele creano all'esterno un ambiente speciale. Sistemale, da sole o dentro delle lanterne, sui gradini delle scale, sul bordo del balcone o agli angoli del patio.

As velas criam um ambiente especial no exterior. Coloque-as individualmente ou dentro de lampiões, nos degraus das escadas, na orla da varanda ou nos cantos do pátio.

Ljus skapar en speciell stämning utomhus. Placera dem fristående eller i lyktor, på trappstegen, vid balkongens kanter eller i uteplatsens hörn.

Recreates a romantic and functional ambience with wrought iron antique beds that can be used as seats or berths to enjoy long naps outdoors.

On peut recréer une atmosphère romantique et fonctionnelle avec des lits anciens en fer forgé faisant office de siège ou de transat pour profiter de longues siestes en plein air.

Gestalten Sie eine romantische und funktionale Umgebung mit alten schmiedeeisernen Betten, die als Sitzmöbel oder Liegen für lange Siestas im Freien dienen.

Schep een romantische en functionele sfeer met enkel oude smeedijzeren bedden die dienst doen als zitplaatsen of ligstoelen, om te genieten van lange siësta's in de buitenlucht.

Recrea un ambiente romántico y funcional con unas camas antiguas de forja que funcionen como asientos o tumbonas para disfrutar de unas largas siestas al aire libre.

Ricrea un ambiente romantico e funzionale con antichi letti in ferro battuto, che potrai utilizzare come sedute o punto relax per lunghi momenti di riposo all'aria aperta.

Recrie um ambiente romântico e funcional com camas antigas em metal forjado que funcionem como bancos ou espreguiçadeiras onde possa desfrutar de longas sestas ao ar livre.

Skapa en romantisk och funktionell miljö med några gamla järnsängar som fungerar som sittplats eller för att njuta av långa tupplurer i det gröna.

Lay rugs outdoors to define ambiences and add warmth and personality to the space.

Sortir les tapis à l'extérieur aide à créer une atmosphère, apporte de la chaleur et personnalise l'espace.

Legen Sie draußen Teppiche aus, um Bereiche abzugrenzen und der Umgebung Wärme und Persönlichkeit zu verleihen.

Haal de vloerkleden naar buiten om ruimtes af te bakenen en voor een warme en persoonlijke sfeer.

Saca las alfombras al exterior para definir ambientes y dar calidez y personalidad al espacio.

Porta fuori i tappeti per definire gli ambienti e dare calore e personalità agli spazi.

Utilize tapetes no exterior para definir áreas e conferir calor e personalidade ao espaço.

Ta mattorna utomhus för att skapa miljöer och skänka värme och personlighet åt platsen.

The creation of exterior points of light is as important as inside the house. Use large lanterns, strings of lights and small spotlights to create a special atmosphere.

L'éclairage est aussi important à l'intérieur qu'à l'extérieur. Grandes lanternes, guirlandes lumineuses et petits lampadaires créent une belle atmosphère.

Die Installation von Lichtquellen ist draußen genauso wichtig wie im Inneren des Hauses. Verwenden Sie große Laternen, Lichterketten und kleine Scheinwerfer, um eine besondere Atmosphäre zu schaffen.

De creatie van lichtpunten is buiten net zo belangrijk als binnenshuis. Kies voor lantaarns, guirlandes en kleine spots om een speciale sfeer te creëren.

La creación de puntos de luz en el exterior es tan importante como dentro de la casa. Echa mano de faroles de gran formato, guirnaldas luminosas y pequeños focos para crear un ambiente especial.

La creazione di punti luce all'esterno è importante sia all'interno che all'esterno della casa. Usa delle grandi lanterne, ghirlande luminose e piccoli punti luce per creare un ambiente speciale.

A criação de pontos de luz no exterior é tão importante como interior da casa. Recorra a lampiões de grande dimensão, candeias e pequenos focos para criar um ambiente especial.

Att skapa ljuspunkter är lika viktigt utomhus som inomhus. Använd stora lyktor, små papperslyktor och små spotlights för att skapa en specieli stämning.

Make use of the slope in the yard to create chill out spaces with cushions on the steps.

Vous pouvez utiliser le dénivelé de la cour pour créer un espace de détente avec des coussins sur les marches.

Profitieren Sie von den Höhenunterschieden im Patio, um mit Kissen auf den Treppenstufen einen *chill out* Bereich zu schaffen.

Benut hoogteverschillen in de patio voor een *chill out* ruimte met kussens op de traptreden.

Aprovecha el desnivel en el patio para crear un espacio *chill out* con cojines en los escalones.

Sfrutta il dislivello del patio per creare uno spazio *chill out* con cuscini posti sui gradini.

Aproveite o desnível no pátio para criar um espaço *chill out* com almofadas nos degraus.

Använd uteplatsens nivåskillnad för att skapa ett "chillout"-område med kuddar på trappstegen.

There is no exterior space, regardless of its size, that cannot be transformed into a small, individual Eden with a pergola and a retractable awning.

Quelle que soit sa dimension, tout espace extérieur peut devenir un petit paradis privé grâce à une pergola ou à une véranda rétractable.

Es gibt keinen Außenraum, unabhängig von seiner Größe, der nicht durch eine Pergola und eine einziehbare Markise in ein kleines Paradies verwandelt werden kann.

Alle buitenruimtes kunnen, ongeacht de grootte, worden omgebouwd tot een klein privé-paradijs door middel van een pergola en een zonnescherm.

No existe un espacio exterior, independientemente de su tamaño, que no pueda ser transformado en un pequeño edén particular mediante una pérgola y un toldo retráctil.

Non esiste uno spazio esterno, indipendentemente dalle sue dimensioni, che non possa essere trasformato in un piccolo paradiso grazie a una pergola o a una copertura retrattile.

Não existe um espaço exterior, independentemente do seu tamanho, que não possa ser transformado num pequeno paraíso privado através de uma pérgula e de um toldo retráctil.

Alla trädgårdar, oavsett storlek, kan förvandlas till ett personligt paradis med en pergola och ett ihopfällbart solskydd.

Recliners with a reclining back are perfect for sunbathing on the balcony throughout the year. Add a floor lamp exterior to create a reading area at night.

Les chaises longues avec dossier inclinable sont parfaites pour profiter du soleil sur le balcon pendant toute l'année. Si vous ajoutez un lampadaire d'extérieur, vous créez une zone de lecture pour le soir.

Liegen mit verstellbarer Rückenlehne sind perfekt dazu geeignet, sich zu jeder Jahreszeit auf dem Balkon zu sonnen. Stellen Sie eine Außenstehlampe daneben, um einen Lesebereich für den Abend zu schaffen.

Ligstoelen met verstelbare leuning zijn perfect om het hele jaar door van de zon op het balkon te genieten. Combineer ze met een staande buitenlamp voor een leeszone 's avonds.

Las tumbonas con respaldo reclinable son perfectas para aprovechar el sol en el balcón durante todo el año. Acompáñalas con una lámpara de pie de exterior para crear una zona de lectura para la noche.

I lettini con schienale reclinabile sono perfetti per godersi il sole sul balcone tutto l'anno. Accompagnali con una lampada a pavimento da esterni per creare una zona di lettura serale.

As espreguiçadeiras com encosto reclinável são perfeitas para aproveitar o sol na varanda durante todo o ano. Acrescente um candeeiro de pé de exterior para criar uma zona de leitura à noite.

Liggstolar med fällbart ryggstöd är perfekta för att njuta av solen på balkongen året runt. Placera dem bredvid en golvlampa för utomhusbruk och du har en plats för kvällsläsning.

TEXTURE AND COLOR
MATIÈRES ET COULEURS
TEXTUR UND FARBE
TEXTUUR EN KLEUR
TEXTURA Y COLOR
MATERIALI E COLORI
TEXTURA E COR
TEXTUR OCH FÄRG

Let the walls of your house reveal your personality and flood the house with color.

Vous pouvez laisser votre personnalité s'exprimer, en osant la couleur sur les murs de la maison.

Lassen Sie die Wände Ihres Hauses sprechen und trauen Sie sich, die Wohnung in Farbe zu tauchen.

Laat de muren van uw huis een spreekbuis voor u zijn en durf de woning onder te dompelen in kleur.

Deja que los muros de tu casa hablen de ti y atrévete a inundar la vivienda de color.

Lascia che le pareti della tua casa parlino di te, inonda gli ambienti di colore.

Deixe que as paredes do seu lar falem por si e atreva-se a inundar a casa de cor.

Låt väggarna i ditt hem representera dig och våga använda färg i ditt hem.

Warm colors such as red and yellow, are stimulating, dynamic and happy. They also provide warmth, enhance light and visually bring the walls closer together.

Les tonalités chaudes, du rouge au jaune, sont stimulantes, vitales et joyeuses. Elles apportent aussi une sensation de chaleur, renforcent la lumière et rapprochent visuellement les murs.

Warme Töne von Rot bis Gelb sind anregend, lebendig und fröhlich. Sie vermitteln ein Gefühl von Wärme, verstärken das Licht und lassen die Wände näher wirken.

Warme tonen, vanaf rood tot geel, zijn stimulerend, vitaal en vrolijk. Ook roepen ze een gevoel van warmte op, versterken ze het licht en brengen ze de muren visueel dichterbij.

Los tonos cálidos, del el rojo al amarillo, son estimulantes, vitales y alegres. También aportan sensación de calor, potencian la luz y acercan visualmente las paredes.

I toni caldi, dal rosso al giallo, sono stimolanti, vitali e allegri. Trasmettono inoltre calore, potenziano la luce e avvicinano visivamente le pareti.

Os tons quentes, desde o vermelho ao amarelo, são estimulantes, vitais e alegres. Transmitem uma sensação de calor, potenciam a luz e aproximam visualmente as paredes.

Varma toner, från rött till gult, är stimulerande, vitala och glada. De ger också en känsla av värme, förstärker ljuset och närmar väggarna visuellt.

Red and orange colors are recommended for large spaces or to make one wall stand out. Orange is a color that conveys a sense of well-being.

Le rouge et l'orange sont indiqués pour des surfaces très vastes ou faire ressortir un mur. L'orange, en particulier, transmet la sensation de bienêtre.

Rot und Orange sind empfehlenswerte Farben für große Räume oder um eine Wand hervorzuheben. Orange hat die Eigenschaft, Wohlbefinden zu vermitteln.

Rode en oranje kleuren zijn aan te bevelen voor grote ruimtes of om een muur te laten opvallen. Oranje heeft als bijzonderheid dat er een gevoel van welzijn uit spreekt.

Los colores rojos y naranjas son aconsejables para espacios amplios o para destacar una pared. El naranja tiene la particularidad de transmitir sensación de bienestar.

I colori rosso e arancio sono consigliabili per gli spazi grandi o per dare risalto a una parete. L'arancio ha la caratteristica di trasmettere la sensazione di benessere.

As cores vermelhas e laranjas são aconselháveis para espaços amplos ou para realçar uma parede. A cor laranja tem a particularidade de transmitir a sensação de bem-estar.

Rött och orange är lämpligt för stora rum eller för att utmärka en vägg. Orange har den speciella egenskapen att den ger en känsla av välbehag.

Environments with strong colors like red or orange must strike a balance with light and preferably plain colors.

Vous pouvez équilibrer des couleurs fortes comme le rouge et l'orange par la présence de couleurs claires et de préférence unies.

In Bereichen mit starken Farben wie Rot oder Orange muss man einen Ausgleich mit hellen, Farben, vorzugsweise ohne Muster, schaffen.

Zorg in ruimtes met felle kleuren zoals rood of oranje voor een evenwicht met heldere en bij voorkeur effen kleuren.

En ambientes con colores fuertes como el rojo o el naranja hay que crear un equilibrio con colores claros y preferentemente lisos.

Negli ambienti in cui sono presenti colori forti come il rosso o l'arancio occorre creare un equilibrio con colori chiari e preferibilmente senza fantasie.

Em ambientes com cores fortes como vermelho ou laranja é necessário criar um equilíbrio com cores claras e de preferência lisas.

I rum med starka färger som rött och orange måste man skapa balans med ljusa färger, helst enfärgade.

Yellows, browns and mustard are stimulating and create a feeling of warmth. Use them if you live in a cold area or the room does not receive much sunlight.

Les couleurs jaune, ocre et moutarde sont stimulantes et génèrent une sensation de chaleur. Elles sont particulièrement adaptées aux régions froides ou aux pièces assez sombres.

Gelb, Ocker und Senf sind anregend und schaffen eine warme Atmosphäre. Verwenden Sie sie, wenn sie in einem kalten Gebiet wohnen, oder das Zimmer nicht viel Sonnenlicht empfängt.

Gele, oker en mosterdtinten zijn stimulerend en geven een gevoel van warmte. Gebruik ze als u in een koud gebied woont of als de kamer niet veel zonlicht krijgt.

Los amarillos, ocres y mostazas son estimulantes y generan una sensación de calor. Empléalos si vives en una zona fría o si la habitación no recibe mucha luz solar.

I colori giallo, ocra e mostarda sono stimolanti e generano una sensazione di calore. Utilizzali se vivi in una zona fredda o se la stanza non riceve molta luce solare.

Os amarelos, ocres e mostardas são estimulantes e geram uma sensação de calor. Utilize estas cores caso viva numa zona fria ou se a casa receber pouca luz solar.

Gula nyanser, ockra och senap är stimulerande och skapar en känsla av värme. Använd dem om du bor i ett kallt område eller om rummet inte har mycket solljus.

Apply a different color to one of the surfaces that forms part of the same ambience to highlight structural objects or simply to liven up the room.

Appliquer une couleur différente à l'une des surfaces d'un même environnement fait ressortir les éléments structuraux ou tout simplement donne plus de vie à l'espace.

Gestalten Sie eine der Flächen, die zur selben Umgebung gehören in einer anderen Farbe, um strukturelle Objekte hervorzuheben oder einfach um den Raum lebendiger wirken zu lassen.

Breng een verschillende kleur aan op een van de oppervlaktes die deel uitmaken van dezelfde ruimte om structurele voorwerpen te laten opvallen of om simpelweg meer levendigheid aan het vertrek te geven.

Aplica un color diferente a una de las superficies que forman parte de un mismo ambiente para resaltar objetos estructurales o simplemente darle más vida a la estancia.

Applica un colore diverso su una delle superfici che costituiscono uno stesso ambiente per dare risalto agli oggetti strutturali o semplicemente vivacizzare l'ambiente.

Aplique uma cor diferente numas das superfícies que fazem parte de um mesmo espaço para realçar objectos estruturais ou simplesmente para dar mais vida ao local.

Applicera en annorlunda färg på en av ytorna i rummet för att utmärka strukturella föremål eller helt enkelt ge rummet mer liv.

Cold colors such as green are ideal to "cool down" a south-facing room or a room that is too warm or small.

Les couleurs froides comme le vert sont idéales pour « refroidir » une pièce orientée plein sud ou trop chaude et de dimensions réduites.

Kalte Farben, wie Grün, sind ideal um ein Zimmer, das nach Süden liegt, oder zu warm und klein ist, «abzukühlen».

Koude kleuren zoals groen zijn ideaal om een kamer op het zuiden of een te warme en kleine kamer «af te koelen».

Los colores fríos como el verde son ideales para «enfriar» una habitación con orientación sur o demasiado cálida y de reducido tamaño.

I colori freddi come il verde sono perfetti per "raffreddare" una stanza orientata a sud, troppo calda o di dimensioni ristrette.

As cores frias como o verde são ideais para «arrefecer» um quarto com orientação a sul ou demasiado quente e de dimensões reduzidas.

Kalla färger som t.ex. grönt är idealiska för att "kyla ned" ett rum i som ligger i söderläge eller som är för varmt och litet.

For a high ceiling to seem lower it should be painted the same color as the walls.

Pour abaisser visuellement un plafond très haut, il faut le peindre de la même couleur que les murs.

Damit eine hohe Decke niedriger wirkt, sollte man sie in derselben Farbe wie die Wände streichen.

Verf een hoog plafond, om het lager te laten lijken, in dezelfde kleur als de muren.

Para que un techo alto parezca más bajo se debe pintar del mismo color que las paredes.

Per abbassare visivamente un soffitto alto, sarà necessario dipingerlo nello stesso colore delle pareti.

Para que um tecto alto pareça mais baixo deverá ser pintado da mesma cor que as paredes.

För att ett högt tak ska verka lägre kan man måla det i samma färg som väggarna.

Color can establish a focal point or create interest in a point of the room, whether it is through painting a wall a different color or through elements such as curtains or rugs.

La couleur permet d'attirer l'attention sur un endroit précis de la maison, par exemple un mur peint d'une couleur différente ou des éléments comme les rideaux ou les tapis.

Die Farbe kann einen Blickpunkt bieten oder das Interesse auf eine Stelle des Zimmers lenken, entweder durch eine Wand in einer anderen Farbe oder durch Elemente wie Vorhänge oder Teppiche.

Kleur kan de aandacht vestigen op een bepaald punt in de kamer. Dat effect kan zowel bereikt worden door een muur in een andere kleur te verven als door middel van elementen zoals gordijnen of vloerkleden.

El color puede establecer un punto focal o crear interés en un punto de la habitación, ya sea pintando una pared de un color diferente o a través de elementos como las cortinas o las alfombras.

Il colore può definire un punto focale o creare interesse in un punto della stanza, sia dipingendo una parete di un colore diverso che utilizzando elementi come tende o tappeti.

A cor pode estabelecer um ponto de convergência ou centrar as atenções numa parte do espaço. Isto pode ser conseguido pintando uma parede de uma cor diferente ou através de elementos como as cortinas ou os tapetes.

Färgen kan etablera en fokuspunkt eller skapa intresse för en punkt i rummet, antingen genom att måla en vägg i en annan färg eller genom element som gardiner och mattor.

Using two different colors for walls can achieve interesting results: generating amplitude, visually reducing a space or highlighting a corner.

Peindre deux murs avec deux couleurs différentes permet d'obtenir des résultats intéressants : élargir visuellement l'espace, le réduire ou faire ressortir un angle.

Wenn man zwei Farben für verschiedene Wände benutzt, kann man interessante Ergebnisse erzielen: Weite schaffen, einen Raum kleiner wirken lassen oder eine Ecke hervorheben.

Het gebruik van twee kleuren voor verschillende wanden kan interessante resultaten opleveren: meer ruimte, om een ruimte kleiner te laten lijken of om de aandacht te vestigen op een bepaald hoekje.

Al usar dos colores para diferentes paredes se pueden lograr resultados interesantes: generar amplitud, reducir visualmente un espacio o destacar un rincón.

Utilizzando due colori per pareti diverse è possibile ottenere risultati interessanti: generare senso di ampiezza, ridurre visivamente uno spazio o mettere in risalto un angolo.

Ao usar duas cores para diferentes paredes é possível obter resultados interessantes: criar amplitude, reduzir visualmente um espaço ou dar destaque a uma zona.

Om man använder två färger på olika väggar kan man skapa intressanta resultat: skapa utrymme, förminska synintrycket av ett utrymme eller framhäva en hörna.

Architectural features such as moldings are accentuated when painted a darker or lighter color than the walls.

Les éléments architecturaux, telles les moulures, ressortent du cadre en les peignant avec une couleur plus sombre ou plus claire que le mur.

Architektonische Besonderheiten wie Zierleisten werden hervorgehoben, wenn man sie in einer dunkleren oder helleren Farbe als die Wände streicht.

Bouwkundige kenmerken zoals lijstwerken worden geaccentueerd als ze in een donkerdere of juist lichtere kleur dan de muren worden geschilderd.

Las características arquitectónicas tales como las molduras se acentúan cuando se pintan de un color más oscuro o más ligero que las paredes.

Le caratteristiche architettoniche come le modanature vengono accentuate se colorate in toni più scuri o più chiari rispetto alle pareti.

As características arquitectónicas como as molduras ganham destaque quando pintadas de uma cor mais escura ou mais clara que as paredes.

Speciella arkitektoniska drag som gipslister kan framhävas genom att man målar dem i en mörkare eller ljusare färg än väggarna.

If you go for a dark color for the wall, make sure the room is well-lit. If not, it will seem cold and small.

Vous pouvez peindre un mur avec une couleur sombre si la pièce est bien éclairée, sinon elle paraîtra très peu accueillante et semblera plus petite.

Wenn Sie sich für eine dunkle Wandfarbe entscheiden, sorgen Sie dafür, dass das Zimmer gut beleuchtet ist. Wenn nicht, wirkt es ungemütlich und wirkt kleiner.

Kiest u voor een donkere kleur op de muur, doe dat dan in een goed verlichte kamer, anders lijkt hij ongezellig en klein.

Si te decantas por un color oscuro para la pared, procura que se trate de una habitación bien iluminada. De lo contrario, resultará poco acogedora y parecerá más pequeña.

Se desideri applicare un colore scuro a una parete, scegli una stanza ben illuminata, altrimenti otterresti un ambiente poco accogliente e visivamente più piccolo.

Caso opte por uma cor escura para a parede, é recomendável que se trate de um espaço bem iluminado. Caso contrário, o espaço em causa ficará pouco acolhedor e parecerá mais pequeno.

Om du väljer en mörk färg på väggarna så bör rummet ha mycket dagsljus. I motsatt fall kommer det inte att verka hemtrevligt och kännas mindre.

Microcement is suitable for all types of surfaces and can be applied over any covering. It is available in a wide range of colors, it does not require sealing and is easily cleaned.

Le microciment est adapté à tout type de surface et peut être posé sur n'importe quel revêtement. Il présente une vaste gamme de couleurs, n'a pas de jointures et est très facile à nettoyer.

Mikrozement ist für alle Arten von Oberflächen geeignet und kann auf jeden Verputz aufgetragen werden. Es gibt ihn in vielen verschiedenen Farben, er erfordert keine Fugen und ist leicht zu reinigen.

Microcement is geschikt voor alle soorten oppervlakken en kan op ieder willekeurige bekleding worden toegepast. Er is een breed kleurengamma voorhanden, er zijn geen voegnaden nodig en het is eenvoudig schoon te maken.

El microcemento es apto para todo tipo de superficies y se puede aplicar por encima de cualquier revestimiento. Tiene una amplia gama de colores, no requiere de juntas y es de fácil limpieza.

Il microcemento si presta per qualsiasi tipo di superficie e può essere applicato su qualsiasi rivestimento. È disponibile in un'ampia gamma di colori, non richiede giunzioni ed è facile da pulire.

O microcimento é adequado para todo o tipo de superfícies e pode ser aplicado por cima de qualquer revestimento. Existe uma ampla gama de cores, é de aplicação uniforme e de fácil limpeza.

Mikrocement är lämpligt för alla typer av ytor och det kan appliceras ovanpå alla typer av underlag. Det finns i ett stort utbud färger, kräver inga skarvar och är lätt att göra rent.

Traditionally used on roofs, slate is now being used on walls even on the interior due to its elegance and easy maintenance.

Traditionnellement très employée pour réaliser des toitures, l'ardoise est utilisée aujourd'hui aussi sur les murs intérieurs, car elle est élégante et facile à entretenir.

Traditionell oft für Dächer gebraucht, wird Schiefer dank seiner Eleganz und einfachen Wartung auch für Wände, sogar in Innenräumen gebraucht.

Leisteen wordt van oudsher veel gebruikt op daken, maar het gebruik daarvan heeft zich uitgebreid tot muren en zelfs binnenshuis dankzij de elegantie en doordat het onderhoudsvriendelijk is.

Tradicionalmente muy utilizada en tejados, la pizarra se ha extendido a paredes, incluso en el interior, gracias a su elegancia y el fácil mantenimiento.

Tradizionalmente molto utilizzata per la realizzazione di tetti, la lavagna oggi è usata anche negli ambienti interni grazie alla sua eleganza e alla facile manutenzione.

Tradicionalmente muita utilizada em telhados, a aplicação da lousa estendeu-se às paredes, inclusivamente em interiores graças à sua elegância e fácil manutenção.

Det har traditionellt använts till tak, men skiffer har kommit att användas till inomhusväggar på grund av sin elegans och sitt enkla underhåll.

Stone cladding is no longer synonymous with rustic style. The application of the latest technology gives the porcelain interesting natural stone effects and resistance.

Utiliser la pierre pour revêtir une surface n'est plus synonyme de style rustique. Les dernières technologies confèrent au grès porcelainé des effets intéressants, rappelant la pierre naturelle, et une grande résistance.

Steinbeschichtung ist nicht mehr gleichbedeutend mit rustikalem Stil. Die Verwendung neuester Technologien verleiht Feinsteingut interessante Natursteineffekte und große Widerstandskraft.

Bekleden met steen is niet meer synoniem met een landelijke stijl. De toepassing van de laatste technologieën zorgt ervoor dat aardewerk interessante effecten van natuursteen kan geven en zeer duurzaam is.

Revestir con piedra ya no es sinónimo de estilo rústico. La aplicación de las últimas tecnologías otorga al gres porcelánico interesantes efectos de piedra natural y una gran resistencia.

Scegliere un rivestimento in pietra non è più sinonimo di stile rustico. L'applicazione delle più recenti tecnologie consente di ottenere con il gres porcellanato degli effetti in pietra naturale e una grande resistenza.

Revestir com pedra já não é sinónimo de estilo rústico. A aplicação das mais recentes tecnologias confere ao grés porcelânico interessantes efeitos de pedra natural e uma grande resistência.

Att täcka väggarna med sten är inte längre synonymt med en rustik stil. Tillämpningen av de senaste teknologierna ger keramiskt stengods intressanta effekter som liknar natursten och stor hållbarhet.

Marble is both an elegance and timeless finish. In the kitchen, achieve a striking aesthetic effect by covering the walls and worktops with the same type of marble.

Le marbre apporte une touche très élégante et est toujours à la mode. L'utilisation du même type de marbre sur les murs et les plans de travail de la cuisine permet d'obtenir un effet esthétique saisissant.

Marmor sieht sehr elegant aus und kommt nie aus der Mode. Erreichen Sie in der Küche einen ästhetischen Eindruck, indem Sie die Wände und die Arbeitsflächen mit derselben Marmorart verkleiden.

Marmer geeft een zeer elegante afwerking en raakt nooit uit de mode. In de keuken bereikt u een indrukwekkend esthetisch effect door de muren en werkbladen met hetzelfde type marmer te bekleden.

El mármol aporta un acabado de gran elegancia y no pasa de moda. En la cocina, consigue un impactante efecto estético revistiendo las paredes y encimeras del mismo tipo de mármol.

Il marmo è una finitura di grande eleganza che non passa mai di moda. In cucina consente di ottenere un effetto estetico di grande impatto, con il rivestimento di pareti e ripiani utilizzando lo stesso tipo di materiale.

O mármore confere um acabamento de grande elegância e não passa de moda. Na cozinha, é possível obter um efeito estético de grande impacto ao utilizar o mesmo tipo de mármore no revestimento de paredes e bancadas.

Marmor är ett mycket elegant ytmaterial som aldrig blir omodernt. I köket kan du skapa en imponerande estetisk effekt genom att klä väggarna och arbetsytorna i samma typ av marmor.

When deciding on the colors for the walls and furniture, take into account the flooring. Brown-toned flooring will not go well with certain colors for walls and ceilings.

Dans le choix de la couleur des murs et des meubles, on doit tenir compte du sol. Un revêtement dans les tons bruns ne s'accordera pas trop aux murs et à un plafond aux couleurs multiples.

Berücksichtigen Sie den Boden, wenn Sie die Farbe der Wände und der Möbel wählen. Ein Boden in Brauntönen passt nicht allzugut zu mehrfarbigen Wänden und Decken.

Let bij de keuze van de kleur voor muren en meubels op de vloer. Een vloer in bruine tinten doet het niet goed bij muren en plafonds in diverse kleuren.

Ten en cuenta el suelo a la hora de decidir el color de las paredes y los muebles. Un suelo de tonos marrones no irá demasiado bien con paredes y techos de múltiples colores.

È importante tenere conto del pavimento quando si decide il colore di pareti e mobili. Un pavimento nei toni del marrone non si combinerà bene con pareti e soffitti multi-colore.

Há que ter em conta o pavimento no momento de escolher a cor das paredes e dos móveis. Um pavimento de tons castanhos não será o mais indicado para paredes e tectos com múltiplas cores.

Tänk på golvet när du väljer färg på väggarna och möblerna. Ett golv i bruna nyanser går inte så bra ihop med väggar och tak i olika färger.

To get a sense of continuity between the kitchen and the dining room, choose a single light-colored flooring for both environments. Oak is the hardest and most hard-wearing wood.

Pour obtenir une sensation de continuité entre la cuisine ouverte et la salle à manger, il faut choisir pour le sol un seul type de revêtement de ton clair. Le chêne est un bois très dur et résistant.

Um ein Gefühl von Einheitlichkeit von offener Küche und Esszimmer zu erreichen, wählen Sie für beide Bereiche einen einzigen Bodenbelag in hellen Tönen. Eiche ist das härteste und widerstandsfähigste Holz.

Kies, om een gevoel van doorlopendheid tussen de open keuken en de eetkamer over te dragen, voor een soort plavuizen in een licht tint voor beide ruimtes. Eikenhout is de hardste en duurzaamste houtsoort.

Para conseguir una sensación de continuidad entre la cocina abierta y el comedor, elige un único pavimento de tonos claros para ambos ambientes. El roble es la madera más dura y resistente.

Per ottenere una sensazione di continuità tra la cucina aperta e la sala da pranzo, conviene optare per un unico pavimento chiaro che abbracci entrambi gli ambienti. Il rovere è il legno più duro e resistente

Para conseguir uma sensação de continuidade entre a cozinha aberta e sala de jantar, escolha um único pavimento de tons claros para ambos os espaços. O carvalho é a madeira mais sólida e resistente.

För att skapa en känsla av kontinuitet mellan det öppna köket och matsalen, bör du välja ett och samma golv i ljusa färger i båda rummen. Ek är det hårdaste och tåligaste golvet.

One way to soften the rustic tone of the exposed brick is to paint it white and combine it with natural wood tones.

Le côté rustique de la brique peut être nuancé en la peignant en blanc et en l'associant à des bois aux tons naturels.

Eine Art, den rustikalen Eindruck von sichtbaren Ziegelsteinen zu mildern, ist, sie weiß zu streichen und mit Holz in Naturtönen zu verbinden.

Een manier om het landelijke accent van onbepleisterde baksteen te verminderen, is om het wit te schilderen en te combineren met hout in natuurlijke tinten.

Una forma de suavizar el acento rústico del ladrillo a la vista es pintarlo de color blanco y combinarlo con madera en tonos naturales.

Un modo per smorzare l'accento rustico della mattonella a vista è dipingerla di bianco e combinarla con un legno nei toni naturali.

Uma forma de suavizar o aspecto rústico do tijolo à vista é pintá-lo de cor branca e combiná-lo com madeira em tons naturais.

Ett sätt att mjuka upp den rustika känslan av tegel är att måla det vitt och kombinera det med trä i ljusa färger.

Roofs with wooded or metal beams can become
an additional decorative element if they are painted
to match the rest of the room.

Les plafonds à poutres en bois ou en métal peints avec
une couleur qui s'accorde avec le reste de la pièce
peuvent devenir un élément de décoration.

Decken aus Holz- oder Metallbalken können in ein
zusätzliches dekoratives Element verwandelt werden,
wenn man sie in einer Farbe, die dem übrigen Zimmer
entspricht, streicht.

Plafonds van houten of metalen balken kunnen een
decoratief element worden als ze worden geschilderd
in een kleur die past bij de rest van de kamer.

Los techos de vigas de madera o metal pueden
convertirse en un elemento decorativo adicional
se si los pinta de un color acorde al resto de la
habitación.

I soffitti a travi di legno o metallo possono trasformarsi
in un elemento decorativo aggiuntivo se vi si applica del
colore, in tono con il resto della stanza.

Os tectos com vigas de madeira ou metal podem ser
convertido num elemento decorativo adicional se forem
pintados de uma cor em concordância com o resto
do espaço.

Trä- eller metallbjälkar i taket kan bli ett dekorativt inslag
om man målar dem i en färg som passar ihop med resten
av rummet.

Dark colors can only be used to clad both the walls and ceiling if there is a large window to ensure that light enters.

Une pièce ayant le même revêtement aux murs et au plafond ne supportera les tons sombres que si elle a de grandes fenêtres assurant l'accès de la lumière.

Ein Zimmer mit derselben Auskleidung an den Wänden und an der Decke erlaubt nur dann dunkle Töne, wenn es große Fenster hat, die Licht einlassen.

Een vertrek met dezelfde bekleding op de wanden als het plafond kan donker van kleur zijn als ze grote ramen hebben waardoor de lichtinval gegarandeerd wordt.

Una habitación con el mismo revestimiento en las paredes y el techo admite tonos oscuros solo si cuenta con grandes ventanas que aseguren la entrada de la luz.

Una camera con lo stesso rivestimento su pareti e soffitto consente solo l'impiego di toni scuri se dispone di grandi finestre che garantiscano l'ingresso della luce.

Um espaço com o mesmo revestimento nas paredes e no tecto só pode ser realizado em tons escuros caso existam grandes janelas que assegurem a entrada da luz.

Ett rum med samma beläggning på väggarna som i taket kan bara målas i mörka färger om det har stora fönster som garanterar ljusinsläpp.

To convey a sense of balance, combine floors with different colors with furniture and fabric in the same color range.

Pour transmettre une sensation d'équilibre, le carrelage du sol avec plusieurs couleurs doit s'harmoniser avec des meubles et des textiles appartenant à la même gamme de couleur.

Um einen Eindruck von Ausgeglichenheit zu vermitteln, richten Sie die Zimmer, die Böden aus verschiedenfarbigen Fliesen haben, mit Möbeln und Textilien der gleichen Farbskala ein.

Om een gevoel van evenwicht over te dragen kunt u de kamers uitrusten met tegelvloeren in verschillende kleuren, meubels en stoffering binnen hetzelfde kleurengamma.

Para transmitir una sensación de equilibrio, equipa las habitaciones con suelos de baldosas de diferentes colores, con muebles y textiles de una misma gama de color.

Per trasmettere una sensazione di equilibrio, optare per pavimenti con piastrelle di colori diversi con mobili e tessuti di una stessa gamma tonale.

Para transmitir uma sensação de equilíbrio, equipe os quartos com pavimentos em ladrilhos de diferentes cores com móveis e têxteis de uma mesma gama de cor.

För att skapa en känsla av balans bör man inreda rum som har golvplattor i olika nyanser med möbler och textiler i en färgskala.

If the flooring in a room is black the walls and ceilings should be white to enhance the feeling of spaciousness.

Si la pièce a un sol noir, les parois et le plafond doivent être peints en blanc, pour augmenter la sensation d'espace.

In Räumen mit schwarzem Boden, ist es günstig, wenn Wände und Decke weiß sind, um einen weiträumigen Eindruck zu bewirken.

In kamers met een zwarte vloer is het raadzaam om de muren en het plafond wit te houden, om een gevoel van ruimte te geven.

En habitaciones con el suelo negro conviene que las paredes y el techo sean de color blanco para realzar la sensación de amplitud.

Nelle stanze con il pavimento nero è preferibile che le pareti e il soffitto siano di colore bianco, per aumentare la sensazione di ampiezza.

Em espaços com o pavimento a negro convém que as paredes e o tecto sejam de cor branca para realçar a sensação de amplitude.

I rum med svarta golv bör väggarna och taket vara vita för att skapa en känsla av rymd.

Find the solution that best fits your home. In addition to the traditional claddings, there is an interesting range of materials such as metal and glass bricks.

Si vous recherchez la solution la plus adaptée à votre maison, outre les revêtements traditionnels, il existe une gamme intéressante de matériaux, tels le métal et le béton de verre.

Suchen Sie die Lösung, die für Ihr Haus am geeignetsten ist. Außer den traditionellen Wandverkleidungen gibt es eine interessante Materialpalette wie Metall oder Glasbausteine.

Zoek de oplossing die het meest geschikt is voor uw huis. Naast de traditionele bekledingen bestaat er een interessant gamma van materialen zoals metaal en glasstenen.

Busca la solución que más se adecue a tu casa. Además de los revestimientos tradicionales, existe una gama interesante de materiales, como el metal y los ladrillos de vidrio.

Ricerca la soluzione migliore per la tua casa. Oltre ai rivestimenti tradizionali, esiste una gamma interessante di materiali come il metallo o le mattonelle di vetro

Procure a solução que mais se adapta à sua casa. Além dos revestimentos tradicionais existe uma gama interessante de materiais como o metal e os tijolos de vidro.

Hitta den lösning som passar ditt hem bäst. Förutom de traditionella beläggningsmaterialen finns det ett intressant utbud av material som metall och tegelstenar av glas.

Small ceramic tiles, either square or oblong, add richness to the texture of the wall. Vitrified tiles add metallic sheen.

Les petits carreaux en céramique, carrés ou allongés, enrichissent la texture du mur et, vitrifiés, ils ajoutent une brillance métallisée.

Kleine, quadratische oder längliche Keramikfliesen bereichern die Textur der Wand. Die glasierten Fliesen haben einen metallischen Glanz.

Kleine keramiek tegeltjes verrijken, of ze nu vierkant of langwerpig zijn, de textuur van de wand. Met geëmailleerde tegeltjes wordt een metaalachtige glans verkregen.

Las baldosas pequeñas de cerámica, ya sean cuadradas o alargadas, aportan riqueza a la textura de la pared. Las vitrificadas suman brillos metalizados.

Le piastrelle in ceramica di piccole dimensioni, quadrate o allungate, arricchiscono la parete. Quelle vetrificate aggiunto un tocco di brillantezza metallizzata.

Os ladrilhos pequenos em cerâmica, sejam quadrados ou alongados, conferem riqueza à textura da parede. Os ladrilhos vitrificados adicionam brilhos metalizados.

Små keramikplattor, vare sig de är fyrkantiga eller avlånga, berikar väggens textur. Glaserade plattor ger också ett metalliskt skimmer.

Make the wall with the mirror stand out by cladding it totally different from the rest of the bathroom.

Vous pouvez faire ressortir le mur où le miroir est accroché avec un revêtement radicalement différent du reste de la salle de bain.

Heben Sie die Wand, an der sich der Spiegel befindet, durch deine Verkleidung hervor, die sich radikal von dem übrigen Bad unterscheidet.

Laat de spiegelwand opvallen met een bekleding die radicaal verschilt van de rest van de badkamer.

Haz destacar la pared del espejo con un revestimiento radicalmente diferente al resto del baño.

Dai risalto alla parete dello specchio con un rivestimento radicalmente diverso dal resto del bagno.

Dê destaque à parede do espelho utilizando um revestimento radicalmente diferente do resto da casa de banho.

Framhäv väggen med spegeln genom att klä den i en annorlunda beläggning än resten av badrummet.

All-white bathrooms have little charm. Break the sense of coldness with a pouffe or a black or brown skin rug.

Les salles de bain complètement blanches ont très peu de charme. Vous pouvez casser la sensation de froid qu'elles transmettent avec un pouf ou un tapis en peau noir ou marron.

Vollkommen weiße Bäder sind nicht sehr fröhlich. Unterbrechen Sie den Eindruck von Kälte, den sie ausstrahlen, mit einem Puff aus schwarzem oder braunem Leder, oder einem Teppich.

Helemaal witte badkamers zijn niet erg charmant. Verbreek het koude gevoel die ze uitstralen met een poef of een zwart of bruin leren vloerkleed.

Los baños totalmente blancos tienen muy poco encanto. Rompe la sensación de frialdad que transmiten con un puf o una alfombra de piel negro o marrón.

I bagni completamente bianchi hanno scarso fascino. Rompi la sensazione di freddezza che trasmettono con un puf o un tappeto in pelle nera o marrone.

As casas de banho totalmente brancas são muito pouco interessantes. Quebre a sensação de frio que transmitem com um pufe ou um tapete de pele preto ou castanho.

Badrum helt i vitt har inte mycket charm. Motverka det kalla intrycket med en sittkudde eller en pälsmatta i svart eller brunt.

DECO DETAILS
DÉTAILS DECO
DEKORATIVE DETAILS
DECO DETAILS
DETALLES DECORATIVOS
DETTAGLI DECORATIVI
DETALHES DECORATIVOS
DEKORATIVA DETALJER

Do not be afraid to contrast: if you chose a radical color for the wall, be consistent with the choice of ornaments and bold shaped lamps.

Il ne faut pas avoir peur des contrastes : si vous avez choisi une couleur vive pour le mur, des éléments décoratifs et des lampes aux formes audacieuses confirmeront votre style.

Fürchten Sie keine Kontraste: Wenn Sie eine radikale Farbe für die Wand gewählt haben, seinen Sie bei der Auswahl von gewagten Dekorationsgegenständen und Lampen konsequent.

Vrees niet voor contrast: heeft u gekozen voor een radicale kleur op de muur, wees dan consequent in de keuze voor decoraties en lampen in gewaagde vormen.

No temas a los contrastes: si has elegido un color radical para la pared, sé consecuente con la elección de adornos y lámparas de formas audaces.

Non temere i contrasti: se hai scelto un colore radicale per la parete, sii coerente e opta per arredi e luci dalle forme audaci.

Não tema os contrastes: caso tenha optado por uma cor radical para a parede, seja coerente na escolha de acessórios e candeeiros com formas audazes.

Var inte rädd för kontraster: om du har valt en stark färg på väggen, var konsekvent i valet av prydnadsföremål och lampor i djärva former.

Do not be afraid to contrast: counteract the cold floor with natural fiber seats or cushions and wool throws.

Il ne faut pas avoir peur des contrastes : vous pouvez pallier à la froideur du sol avec des sièges ou des coussins en fibre naturelle et des couvertures en laine.

Fürchten Sie keine Kontraste: Wirken Sie der Fußbodenkälte mit Sitzen oder Kissen aus Naturfasern und Wolldecken entgegen.

Vrees niet voor contrasten: neutraliseer een koude vloer met zittingen of kussens van natuurvezel en wollen dekens.

No temas a los contrastes: contrarresta el frío del suelo con asientos o cojines de fibra natural y mantas de lana.

Non temere i contrasti: contrasta la freddezza del pavimento con sedute o cuscini in fibra naturale e coperte di lana.

Não tema os contrastes: compense o frio do pavimento com bancos ou almofadas de fibra natural e mantas de lã.

Var inte rädd för kontraster: motverka golvets kyla med stolar eller kuddar i naturfiber och filtar i lammull.

If the ornament is very small, combine it with similar pieces of different sizes. This will not take away from its visual impact.

Si l'élément décoratif est très petit, il vaut mieux créer des ensembles avec des pièces similaires de la même taille, car vous risquez de perdre son impact visuel.

Wenn die Ziergegenstände sehr klein sind, ist es günstig, ähnliche Gegenstände verschiedener Größe zu gruppieren. Wenn nicht, verlieren Sie an Ausdruckskraft.

Als een decorstuk heel klein is, is het een idee om een geheel te vormen met gelijksoortige elementen met verschillende afmetingen. Anders vallen ze niet op.

Si el adorno es muy pequeño, conviene hacer conjuntos con piezas similares de diferentes tamaños; de lo contrario, perderá impacto visual.

Se il soprammobile che hai scelto è molto piccolo, conviene creare gruppi con pezzi simili di diverse dimensioni. Altrimenti andrà perso l'impatto visivo dell'oggetto.

Se o elemento decorativo for muito pequeno, é conveniente fazer conjuntos com peças similares de diferentes tamanhos. Caso contrário o impacto visual irá perder-se

Om ett prydnadsföremål är mycket litet kan man skapa samlingar av liknande föremål i olika storlekar, annars förlorar de sin visuella effekt.

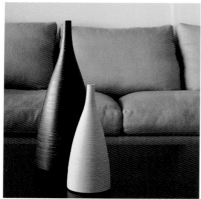

Books can be a decorative element, especially older books. Stack them in order so as they do not seem to have been left there.

Les livres, en particulier s'ils sont anciens, peuvent devenir des objets décoratifs. Il faut juste les empiler d'une manière ordonnée pour qu'ils ne donnent pas l'impression d'avoir été oubliés.

Bücher können sehr dekorativ sein, besonders wenn sie alt sind. Sie sollten nur ordentlich aufgestapelt sein, dass sie nicht so aussehen, als ob man sie vergessen hätte.

Boeken kunnen een decoratief element zijn, vooral als ze oud zijn. Leg ze wel op een nette stapel zodat het niet lijkt alsof ze rondslingeren.

Los libros pueden convertirse en un elemento decorativo, especialmente cuando son antiguos. Solo requieren estar apilados en orden para que no parezca que se han dejado olvidados.

I libri possono trasformarsi in un elemento decorativo, soprattutto quando sono antichi. Basta sistemarli in modo ordinato affinché non diano la sensazione di essere stati dimenticati.

Os livros podem converter-se num elemento decorativo, especialmente quando são antigos. É necessário apenas que sejam dispostos por ordem para que não pareça que foram esquecidos no local.

Böcker kan också fungera som dekorativt element, speciellt om de är gamla. De bör placeras i ordning för att inte ge intryck av att vara bortglömda.

Create a comfy reading corner with a nice bouquet of flowers to help improve mood in a simple and natural way.

On peut créer un coin lecture accueillant grâce à un bouquet de fleurs, qui aide à détendre l'atmosphère avec simplicité et naturel.

Gestalten Sie eine gemütliche Leseecke mit einem hübschen Blumenstrauß, der auf einfache und natürliche Art hilft, die Laune zu heben.

Richt een gezellige leeshoek in met een mooie bos bloemen die op eenvoudige wijze bijdragen aan een goed humeur.

Crea un rincón de lectura acogedor con un buen ramo de flores, que ayudan a mejorar el estado de ánimo de una forma sencilla y natural.

Crea un angolo accogliente per la lettura, con un bel mazzo di fiori che contribuisce a migliorare lo stato d'animo in modo semplice e naturale.

Crie um espaço de leitura acolhedor com um bom ramo de flores. Estas ajudam a melhorar o estado de espírito de uma forma simples e natural.

Skapa en mysig läshörna med en stor blombukett som lyfter humöret på ett enkelt och naturligt sätt.

Use colored glass bottles as vases. Just make sure that they do not have labels or words engraved on the glass, except in the case of very old bottles that could be categorized as vintage.

Les bouteilles en verre coloré peuvent devenir des vases, à condition qu'elles n'aient ni étiquette ni inscription gravée, sauf s'il s'agit de bouteilles très anciennes, qui rentrent dans la catégorie *vintage*.

Verwandeln Sie farbige Glasflaschen in Blumenvasen. Sie dürfen nur keine Etiketten oder ins Glas eingeritzte Worte haben, es sei denn, dass es sich um sehr alte Flaschen handelt, die zur *vintage* Kategorie gehören.

Verander gekleurde glazen flessen in vazen. Het enige vereiste is dat ze geen etiketten of opschriften hebben, tenzij het gaat om hele oude flessen die in de categorie *vintage* vallen.

Convierte en floreros las botellas de vidrio de color. El único requisito es que no tengan etiquetas ni palabras grabadas en el vidrio, salvo que se trate de botellas muy antiguas, que pasan a la categoría de *vintage*.

Trasforma in vaso da fiori le bottiglie di vetro colorate. L'unico requisito è che non abbiano etichette o parole stampate sul vetro, a meno che si tratti di bottiglie molto antiche, classificabili nella categoria *vintage*.

Converta em jarras as garrafas de vidro de coloridas. O único requisito é que não tenham etiquetas nem palavras gravadas no vidro, excepto se se tratarem de garrafas muito antigas que assim passam à categoria de *vintage*.

Använd färgade glasflaskor som blomvaser. Det enda kravet är att de inte bör ha några etiketter eller text i glaset, om de inte är mycket gamla och kan räknas i in kategorin vintage.

Decorate the bathroom with natural elements using a very simple minimalist arrangement such as these single leaves.

Vous pouvez décorer votre salle de bain aves des éléments empruntés à la nature, comme cette composition minimaliste très simple constituée d'une seule feuille.

Dekorieren Sie das Bad mit Elementen aus der Natur mit Hilfe eines minimalistischen, sehr schlichten Arrangement, das nur aus einem großen Blatt besteht.

Decoreer de badkamer met elementen uit de natuur op een minimalistische, eenvoudige manier, met uit een blad.

Adorna el baño con elementos de la naturaleza a través de un arreglo minimalista muy sencillo compuesto solo con una gran hoja.

Arricchisci il bagno con elementi naturali sistemandoli in modo minimalista e semplice, anche solo optando per una grande foglia.

Decore a casa de banho com elementos da natureza através de um arranjo minimalista muito simples composto apenas por uma grande folha.

Smycka badrummet med föremål från naturen, med ett minimalistiskt och enkelt arrangemang som t.ex. kan bestå av ett stort blad.

One decorative option is to combine flowers with the wall paint, upholstery or other objects such as pillows, lamps, curtains and carpets.

Vous pouvez varier la décoration en associant les fleurs à la peinture des murs, à la tapisserie ou à d'autres objets comme coussins, lampes, rideaux et tapis.

Eine dekorative Variante ist, die Blumen mit der Farbe der Wand, den Polsterbezügen oder anderen Gegenständen wie Kissen, Lampen, Vorhängen oder Teppichen zu kombinieren.

Een decoratieve variant is om bloemen te combineren met de kleur verf op de muren, de stoffering of voorwerpen zoals kussens, lampen en vloerkleden.

Una variante decorativa es combinar las flores con la pintura de las paredes, la tapicería u otros objetos, como cojines, lámparas, cortinas y alfombras.

Una variante decorativa è combinare i fiori con le pareti, la tappezzeria o altri oggetti come cuscini, lampade, tende e tappeti.

Uma variante decorativa consiste em combinar as flores com a pintura das paredes, com o revestimento ou com outros objectos como almofadas, candeeiros, cortinados e tapetes.

Ett dekorativt alternativ är att kombinera blommor med färgen på väggarna, textilierna eller andra föremål som kuddar, lampor, gardiner och mattor.

Decorate the windows with prickly pears in small pots attached using a simple metal bar.

Les grandes fenêtres peuvent être décorées avec des plantes grasses dans des petits pots accrochés à une simple barre de métal.

Dekorieren Sie große Fenster mit Kakteen in kleinen Töpfen, die mit Hilfe einer einfachen Metallleiste befestigt werden.

Decoreer grote ramen met vijgencactussen in kleine bloempotten die door middel van een eenvoudige metalen stang worden opgehangen.

Decora las ventanas grandes con tunas en pequeñas macetas que se sujetan a través de una simple barra de metal.

Decora le finestre grandi con cactus sistemati all'interno di piccoli vasi, sostenuti tramite una semplice sbarra in metallo.

Decore as janelas grandes com figueira-da-índia em pequenos vasos que se fixam através de uma simples barra de metal.

Dekorera stora fönster med kaktusar i små krukor som hålls uppe med en enkel metallstång.

Often the composition of a group of decorative objects is more important than the individual piece. Find a balance between the shapes and colors to create charming corners.

Souvent, la composition d'un groupe d'objets décoratifs est plus marquante que la pièce elle-même. La recherche de l'équilibre des formes et des couleurs est fondamentale pour réussir à créer des coins de charme.

Oft ist die Komposition einer Gruppe von dekorativen Gegenständen wichtiger als die einzelnen Stücke. Suchen Sie das Gleichgewicht von Farben und Formen, um charmante Ecken zu gestalten.

De compositie van een groep decoratieve voorwerpen doet vaak meer dan een afzonderlijk element. Zoek naar evenwicht in vormen en kleuren om gezellige hoekjes in te richten.

Muchas veces es más relevante la composición de un grupo de objetos decorativos que las piezas individualmente. Busca el equilibrio de formas y colores para crear rincones con encanto.

Spesso ha un maggiore impatto la composizione di un gruppo di oggetti decorativi che ciascun pezzo singolarmente. Ricerca l'equilibrio di forme e colori per creare angoli affascinanti.

Muitas vezes é mais relevante a composição de um grupo de objectos decorativos que a disposição das peças individualmente. Procure o equilíbrio de formas e cores para criar espaços interessantes.

Ofta är ett arrangemang med en grupp föremål mer intressant än varje enskilt stycke. Hitta balansen mellan former och färger för att skapa charmiga vrår.

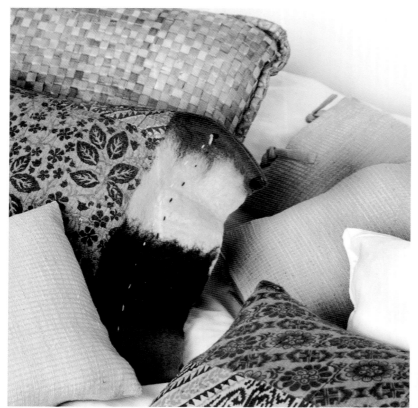

Cushions are a decorative and practical par excellence. In addition to style, comfort and provide the ability to create makeshift seats on the floor.

Les coussins sont les éléments décoratifs et pratiques par excellence. Non seulement ils donnent un style, mais ils apportent aussi du confort et se transforment en sièges improvisés par terre.

Kissen sind dekorative und praktische Elemente schlechthin. Außer zum Stil tragen Sie zur Bequemlichkeit bei und bieten die Möglichkeit, Sitzgelegenheiten auf dem Boden zu improvisieren.

Kussens zijn een decoratief en praktisch element bij uitstek. Behalve stijl geven ze comfort en de mogelijkheid om geïmproviseerde zitplaatsen op de grond te creëren.

Los cojines son los elementos decorativos prácticos por excelencia. Además de estilo, aportan comodidad y la posibilidad de crear asientos improvisados en el suelo.

I cuscini sono un elemento decorativo e pratico per eccellenza. Trasmettono stile, ma anche comodità e consentono di creare sedute improvvisate a terra.

As almofadas são os elementos decorativos e práticos por excelência. Além de estilo, conferem também conforto e a possibilidade de criar assentos improvisados no solo.

Kuddar är ett av de främsta dekorativa och praktiska föremålen i hemmet. Förutom stil tillför de komfort och en möjlighet att skapa improviserade sittplatser på golvet.

Play with combinations of shapes and patterns, but always keep a common pattern, which can be a same range of colors or the same type of textures.

Il est possible de jouer avec les formes et les imprimés, tout en gardant un fil conducteur commun – par exemple, la même gamme de tonalités ou le même type de matière.

Spielen Sie mit der Kombination von Formen und Mustern, aber behalten Sie immer eine gemeinsame Linie bei, die sich in derselben Farbpalette oder in der selben Stoffart ausdrücken kann.

Speel met een combinatie van vormen en opdrukken, maar houd altijd een gemeenschappelijke richtsnoer aan. Dit kan hetzelfde kleurengamma of dezelfde soort textuur.

Juega con las combinaciones de formas y estampados, pero manteniendo siempre una pauta común, que puede ser una misma gama de tonalidades o un mismo tipo de texturas.

Gioca con le combinazioni di forme e stampe, mantenendo sempre uno schema comune, che può essere una stessa gamma tonale o uno stesso tipo di materiale.

Brinque com as combinações de formas e estampados, mas mantendo sempre uma linha comum, que pode ser uma mesma gama de tonalidades ou um mesmo tipo de texturas.

Lek med olika kombinationer av former och mönster, men alltid med en gemensam nämnare, som kan vara en färgskala eller en typ av textur.

Use cushions in the same range of colors to create well-defined spaces in the garden.

Utiliser des coussins dans la même gamme de couleurs permet de créer des espaces bien définis dans le jardin.

Verwenden Sie Kissen derselben Farbskala, um abgegrenzte Bereiche im Garten zu gestalten.

Gebruik kussens in hetzelfde kleurengamma om goed afgebakende ruimtes in de tuin te creëren.

Utiliza cojines de la misma gama de colores para crear espacios bien definidos en el jardín.

Usa i cuscini della stessa gamma cromatica per creare spazi ben definiti in giardino.

Utilize almofadas da mesma gama de cores para criar espaços bem definidos no jardim.

Använd kuddar i samma färgskala för att skapa enhetliga platser i trädgården.

Place comfortable cushions around a low table to create a dining room area outside the house.

Des coussins confortables autour d'une table basse créent un coin repas à l'extérieur de la maison.

Legen Sie ein paar bequeme Kissen auf den Boden um einen niedrigen Tisch herum, und schaffen Sie so einen Essplatz außerhalb des Hauses.

Leg een aantal comfortabele kussens op de grond rondom een laag tafeltje, om buiten een eethoek in te richten.

Sitúa unos cómodos cojines en el sueño alrededor de una mesita baja para crear una zona de comedor en el exterior de la casa.

Posiziona dei comodi cuscini a terra intorno a un tavolino basso per creare una zona per mangiare all'esterno della casa.

Coloque umas almofadas confortáveis no solo em redor de uma mesa baixa para criar uma zona de refeições no exterior da casa.

Placera några bekväma kuddar på marken runt ett lågt bord för att skapa en matplats utomhus.

Frame illustrations, photos or pictures and hang them on the main walls of the house. If you opt for a composition, check it out on the floor before hanging it on the wall.

Vous pouvez encadrer des gravures, des photos ou des dessins et les placer dans les coins clés de la maison. Si vous aimez une composition, il faut l'essayer d'abord au sol.

Rahmen Sie Poster, Fotos oder Bilder und hängen Sie sie an exponierte Wände des Hauses. Wenn Sie sich für eine Komposition entscheiden, probieren Sie sie vorher auf dem Boden aus.

Lijst prenten, foto's of schilderijen in en zet ze langs de belangrijkste muren van het huis. Heeft u een bepaalde compositie in het hoofd, probeer die dan eerst op de vloer uit.

Enmarca láminas, fotos o cuadros y colócalos en paredes claves de la casa. Si te decantas por una composición, pruébala antes sobre el suelo.

Incornicia stampe, foto o quadri e sistemali su pareti chiave della casa. Se opti per una composizione, provala prima sul pavimento.

Emoldure imagens, fotos ou quadros e coloque-os em paredes chave da casa. Caso opte por uma composição, deverá experimentá-la previamente sobre o solo.

Rama in grafiska blad, foton eller tavlor och placera dem på strategiska platser i hemmet. Om du vill göra en komposition kan du pröva att lägga tavlorna på golvet först.

Small and medium pictures tend to visually get lost in the space. It is better integrate them into a composite supported on a desk, shelf or wall overhang.

Les tableaux petits et moyens ont tendance à se perdre visuellement dans l'espace. Il vaut mieux les réunir sur un meuble, une étagère ou un décrochement dans le mur.

Kleine und mittlere Bilder neigen dazu, sich im Raum zu verlieren. Es ist besser sie in einer Gruppe auf einem Möbelstück, in einem Regal oder auf einem Mauervorsprung aufzustellen.

Kleine en middelgrote schilderijen hebben de neiging om in de ruimte onopgemerkt te blijven. Het is dan beter om ze deel uit te laten maken van een compositie, leunend op een meubelstuk, een plank of een richel tegen de muur.

Los cuadros pequeños y medianos tienden a perderse visualmente en el espacio. Mejor integrarlos en una composición apoyados sobre un mueble, un estante o el saliente de la pared.

I quadri di piccole e medie dimensioni tendono a perdersi visivamente nello spazio. È consigliabile integrarli in una composizione, appoggiati su un mobile, un ripiano o una sporgenza della parete.

Os quadros pequenos e médios tendem a perder-se visualmente no espaço. Será melhor integrá-los numa composição apoiados sobre um móvel, uma estante ou sobre uma saliência na parede.

Små och medelstora tavlor har en tendens att försvinna ur synfältet. Det är bättre att låta dem ingå i en komposition som kan lutas mot en möbel, en hylla eller en framskjutande del av väggen.

Enhance the whole concept using the same passe-partout and the same frame.

La notion d'ensemble peut être renforcée en utilisant le même passe-partout et le même cadre.

Verstärken Sie das Ensemble-Konzept, indem Sie gleiche Passepartouts und gleiche Rahmen verwenden.

Versterk het concept van eenheid door gebruik te maken van hetzelfde passepartouts en dezelfde lijst.

Potencia el concepto de conjunto utilizando el mismo paspartú y el mismo marco.

Potenzia il concetto di insieme utilizzando lo stesso passepartout e la stessa cornice.

Realce o conceito de conjunto utilizando a mesma configuração e a mesma moldura.

Förstärk den enhetliga känslan genom att använda samma passepartout och samma ram.

Line up several pictures of the same size, frame and passe-partout to define different environments within a single room.

Des tableaux ayant le même format, cadre et passe-partout peuvent délimiter des espaces consacrés à des usages différents dans une même pièce.

Richten Sie mehrere Bilder von gleicher Größe, mit gleichen Rahmen und gleichem Passepartout in einer Linie aus, um verschiedene Bereiche im Zimmer zu definieren.

Hang verschillende schilderijen met dezelfde afmeting, lijst en passepartouts in een lijn naast elkaar om ruimtes met een verschillend gebruik binnen dezelfde kamer af te bakenen.

Alinea varios cuadros del mismo tamaño, marco y paspartú para definir ambientes de uso diferente dentro de una misma habitación.

Allinea più quadri delle stesse dimensioni, con una stessa cornice o passepartout per definire ambienti di uso diverso all'interno di una stessa stanza.

Alinhe vários quadros com o mesmo tamanho, moldura e configuração para definir zonas com diferentes utilizações dentro do mesmo espaço.

Placera flera tavlor av samma storlek och med samma ram och passepartout tillsammans för att definiera olika användningsområden inom samma rum.

The bathroom, just like any other room in the house, can be decorated and you can hang pictures provided that the walls are not patterned with prints.

On peut décorer la salle de bain comme n'importe quelle autre pièce de la maison : les tableaux sont un excellent choix si les murs n'ont pas de revêtement imprimé.

Das Bad kann man, wie jedes andere Zimmer des Hauses, dekorieren und deshalb kann man dort Bilder aufhängen, vorausgesetzt, dass die Wände keine gemusterten Tapeten haben.

De badkamer kan, net als ieder ander vertrek in het huis, worden gedecoreerd en daarom kunnen er ook schilderijen worden opgehangen, mits de wanden geen bekleding met opdruk hebben.

El baño, como cualquier otra estancia de la casa, se puede decorar, y pueden colgarse allí cuadros siempre y cuando las paredes no tengan un revestimiento estampado.

Il bagno, come qualsiasi altro ambiente della casa, può essere decorato e arredato; se le pareti non hanno rivestimenti stampati, potrai ad esempio appendervi dei quadri.

A casa de banho, como qualquer outro lugar da casa, pode ser decorado e portanto é possível utilizar quadros para o efeito sempre que as paredes não tenham um revestimento estampado.

Badrummet kan dekoreras, liksom övriga rum i huset, och man kan hänga tavlor där, om inte väggarna har en mönstrad tapet.

Why not hang a picture in the kitchen that is not related to the spaces? Find an image that matches the style of the space.

Un tableau au sujet non culinaire assure un effet de surprise dans la cuisine. L'image doit toutefois s'accorder au style de cette pièce.

Schaffen Sie in der Küche mit einem Bild ohne kulinarische Motive einen Überraschungseffekt. Suchen Sie ein Bild, das mit dem Stil dieses Raumes harmoniert.

Verras in de keuken met een schilderij zonder culinaire motieven. Zoek een afbeelding uit die overeenkomt met de stijl van dit vertrek.

Sorprende en la cocina con un cuadro que no tenga motivos culinarios. Busca una imagen que concuerde con el estilo de este espacio.

Sorprendi in cucina con un quadro che non abbia motivi culinari. Ricerca un'immagine che riprenda lo stile di questo ambiente.

Surpreenda na cozinha utilizando um quadro que não tenha motivos culinários. Procure uma imagem que combine com o estilo deste espaço.

Överraska genom att hänga en tavla i köket som inte har kulinariskt motiv. Leta efter en bild som passar rummet stil.

If you have space, take advantage of the worktop to support small pictures but try not to break the harmony of colors in the kitchen.

Si vous avez de la place, vous pouvez poser à côté de l'évier de petits tableaux, respectant l'harmonie des couleurs de la cuisine.

Wenn Sie Platz haben, nutzen Sie die Spüle, um dort kleine Bilder aufzustellen, aber ohne die Farbharmonie der Küche zu unterbrechen

Heeft u ruimte, benut de gootsteen dan als steun voor kleine schilderijen zonder de kleurenharmonie van de keuken te verstoren.

Si cuentas con espacio, aprovecha el fregadero como punto de apoyo de pequeños cuadros pero sin romper con la armonía de colores de la cocina.

Se hai spazio, sfrutta il lavandino come punto di appoggio per piccoli quadri, attenendoti ai colori della cucina.

Caso disponha de espaço, aproveite o lava-louça como ponto de apoio para pequenos quadros mas sem quebrar a harmonia de cores da cozinha.

Om du har plats kan du hänga små tavlor ovanför handfatet, men utan att bryta färgharmonin i köket.

Create a focal point in the room by hanging an image.

Heben Sie die Bedeutung einer Zone eines Zimmers hervor, indem Sie ein Bild dort aufhängen, wohin Sie die Aufmerksamkeit lenken wollen.

Il est possible d'attirer l'attention sur des zones spécifiques de la pièce en les décorant avec une image.

Laat bepaalde delen van een kamer opvallen door er een schilderij op te hangen.

Jerarquiza las zonas de una habitación colocando una imagen allí donde quieras llamar la atención.

Enfatizza le zone di una stanza collocandovi un'immagine nel punto che desideri porre in risalto.

Diferencie as zonas de um quarto colocando uma imagem num local para o qual pretenda chamar a atenção.

Dra uppmärksamheten till en plats i rummet genom att hänga en tavla där.

Mirrors are a great resource when you combine pieces of different styles and periods. The contrast between old and new creates a unique atmosphere.

Les miroirs sont un excellent élément si l'on réunit des pièces d'époques et de styles différents. Le contraste entre l'ancien et le moderne crée une atmosphère unique.

Spiegel bieten ausgezeichnete Möglichkeiten, wenn man Stücke aus verschiedenen Epochen und Stilen kombiniert. Der Kontrast zwischen modern und alt schafft eine einmalige Atmosphäre.

Spiegels zijn een uitstekend hulpmiddel als er verschillende exemplaren uit verschillende periodes en met verschillende stijlen worden gecombineerd. Het contrast tussen modern en antiek zorgt voor een unieke sfeer.

Los espejos son un excelente recurso cuando se combinan piezas de épocas y estilos diferentes. El contraste entre lo moderno y lo antiguo crea un ambiente único.

Gli specchi sono un'ottima soluzione quando si combinano pezzi di epoche e di stili diversi. Il contrasto tra moderno e antico crea un ambiente unico.

Os espelhos são um excelente recurso quando se pretende combinar peças de épocas e estilos diferentes. O contraste entre o moderno e o antigo cria um ambiente único.

Speglar är en utmärkt lösning när de kombineras med antika föremål och olika stilar. Kontrasten mellan modernt och gammalt skapar en unik stämning.

Two full-length mirrors flat leaning against the wall create a sophisticated atmosphere in the bedroom.

Deux miroirs de grande taille posés au sol créent une atmosphère plus sophistiquée dans la chambre à coucher.

Zwei auf dem Boden aufgestellte Ganzkörperspiegel schaffen eine raffinierte Umgebung im Schlafzimmer.

Twee passpiegels op de grond geven een verfijnde sfeer in de slaapkamer.

Dos espejos de cuerpo entero apoyados sobre el suelo crean un ambiente más sofisticado en el dormitorio.

Due specchi a corpo intero appoggiati a terra creano un ambiente più sofisticato in camera.

Dois espelhos de corpo inteiro apoiados sobre o solo criam um ambiente mais sofisticado no quarto.

Två helfigursspeglar som ställs på golvet ger sovrummet ett sofistikerat utseende.

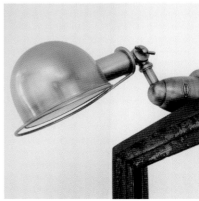

The aesthetic quality of a home depends in part on the individuality of small ornaments that may be antique pieces or from exotic cultures.

La qualité esthétique d'une maison dépend en partie du caractère exclusif de certains objets - pièces anciennes ou provenant de cultures exotiques.

Die ästhetische Qualität eines Hauses hängt zum Teil von der Besonderheit kleiner Dekorationsobjekte ab. Das können antike Stücke oder Gegenstände aus exotischen Kulturen sein.

De esthetische kwaliteit van een woning hangt voor een deel af van de exclusiviteit van kleine decorstukken, zoals antieke voorwerpen of dingen uit exotische culturen.

La calidad estética de una casa depende en parte de la exclusividad de pequeños adornos, que pueden ser piezas antiguas o de culturas exóticas.

L'estetica accogliente di una casa dipende in parte dall'esclusività di piccoli dettagli decorativi come pezzi antichi o esotici.

A qualidade estética de uma casa depende parcialmente da exclusividade de pequenos elementos decorativos, tais como peças antigas ou de culturas exóticas.

Den estetiska kvaliteten hos ett hem beror till stor del på exklusiviteten hos små prydnadsföremål som kan vara gamla stycken eller saker från exotiska kulturer.

Use a personal passion to make it into a decorative
element. Hats, shoes, souvenirs... any object is valid
when it is displayed in an ensemble.

Les passions personnelles peuvent devenir des éléments
de décoration. Chapeaux, chaussures, souvenirs de
voyage... N'importe quel objet peut jouer ce rôle s'il fait
partie d'un ensemble.

Nutzen Sie eine persönliche Leidenschaft für die
Dekoration. Hüte, Schuhe, Reise-souvenirs ... Jeder
Gegenstand ist geeignet, wenn man ihn in einem
Ensemble präsentiert.

Maak van een persoonlijke passie een decoratief
element. Hoeden, schoenen, souvenirs ... alle willekeurig
voorwerpen zijn mogelijk als ze als geheel worden
gepresenteerd.

Utiliza una pasión personal para convertirla en elemento
de decoración. Sombreros, zapatos, souvenirs de viajes...
Cualquier objeto es válido cuando se presenta en un
conjunto.

Mettici passione personale per trasformarla in un
elemento decorativo. Cappelli, scarpe, souvenir di viaggio:
qualsiasi oggetto va bene se presentato all'interno di un
insieme.

Converta uma paixão pessoal num elemento decorativo.
Chapéus, sapatos, souvenirs de viagens... Qualquer
objecto é válido quando enquadrado num conjunto.

Använd dig av ett personligt intresse och använd det som
dekorativt element. Hattar, skor, minnen från resor... vilket
föremål som helst kan användas om det presenteras i en
grupp.

Convert the fireplace shelf into a personal still life of objects of different heights without cluttering the shelf.

L'étagère de la cheminée accueille une nature morte personnelle constituée d'objets de tailles variées, sans toutefois que sa surface soit complètement saturée.

Arrangieren Sie auf dem Kaminsims mit Objekten verschiedener Höhe ein persönliches Stillleben, ohne es zu überladen.

Verander de schoorsteenmantel in een steun voor een persoonlijk stilleven met voorwerpen met verschillende hoogtes, zonder de plank te vol te zetten.

Convierte el estante de la chimenea en el soporte de un bodegón personal con objetos de diferentes alturas, pero sin saturar la balda.

Converti il ripiano del caminetto in supporto dove sistemare oggetti personali di diverse altezze, senza saturare lo spazio.

Converta a estante da lareira no suporte para uma representação de natureza-morta com objectos de diferentes alturas sem saturar o espaço.

Förvandla kaminens hylla till en plats för personliga föremål, utan att överbelamra den.

Candles are a great not only for their decorative appearance but also for the type of light they create.

Les bougies sont de très bons éléments décoratifs, non seulement pour leur apparence mais aussi pour le type d'éclairage qu'elles génèrent.

Kerzen sind sehr dekorativ, nicht nur aufgrund ihres Aussehens, sondern auch wegen der Art des Lichts, das sie erzeugen.

Kaarsen zijn een goede manier om te decoreren, niet alleen vanwege hun uiterlijk, maar ook door het soort verlichting dat ze geven.

Las velas son un muy buen recurso decorativo no solo por su apariencia sino también por el tipo de iluminación que generan.

Le candele sono un'ottima soluzione decorativa, non solo per la loro estetica ma anche per il tipo di illuminazione che producono.

As velas são um elemento decorativo muito bom não só devido à sua estética mas também pelo tipo de iluminação que criam.

Ljus är en bra dekorativ tillgång, inte bara på grund av sitt utseende men också på grund av det ljus de skapar.

* Cuinar v

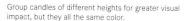

Group candles of different heights for greater visual impact, but they all the same color.

Si vous réunissez des bougies de différentes tailles et de la même couleur, vous obtiendrez un impact visuel plus réussi.

Gruppieren Sie Kerzen von verschiedener Höhe, damit sie auffallen, sie sollten aber alle die gleiche Farbe haben.

Combineer kaarsen van verschillende grootte voor een betere visuele impact, maar houd wel vast aan een kleur.

Agrupa velas de diferentes alturas para un mayor impacto visual, pero que sean todas del mismo color.

Raggruppa candele di diverse altezze per ottenere un maggiore impatto visivo; opta però per un unico colore.

Agrupe velas de diferentes alturas para obter um maior impacto visual, mas apenas se forem todas da mesma cor.

Placera flera ljus av olika höjd tillsammans för ett starkare visuellt intryck, men alla av samma färg.

Hang glass beads from the ceiling lamp, paint words on the curtain, paste vinyl flowers in a corner of the room or use a collection of small objects to give personality to the rooms.

Pour personnaliser les pièces, vous pouvez accrocher des gouttes de verre au lustre, peindre des mots sur les rideaux, coller des stickers au thème floral dans un coin de la chambre à coucher ou utiliser une collection de petits objets.

Hängen Sie Anhänger von Kristallkronleuchtern auf, malen Sie Worte auf die Gardine, kleben Sie Vinylblumen in eine Ecke des Schlafzimmers oder verwenden Sie eine Sammlung kleiner Objekte dafür, diesen Zimmern eine persönliche Atmosphäre zu verleihen.

Hang glazen kralen aan de plafondlamp, teken woorden op het gordijn, plak vinyl bloemen in een hoekje van de slaapkamer of gebruik een collectie kleine voorwerpen om de vertrekken persoonlijk te maken.

Cuelga cuentas de cristal de la lámpara de techo, pinta palabras en la cortina, pega flores de vinilo en un rincón del dormitorio o usa una colección de pequeños objetos para dar personalidad a las estancias.

Appendi gocce di vetro o cristallo al lampadario a soffitto, arricchisci le tende scrivendovi sopra delle parole, attacca dei fiori in vinile in un angolo della camera oppure usa una collezione di piccoli oggetti per personalizzare gli ambienti.

Suspenda contas de vidro no candeeiro de tecto, pinte palavras na cortina, cole flores de vinil numa zona do quarto ou use uma colecção de pequenos objectos para dar personalidade aos espaços.

Häng glaspärlor från taklampan, måla ord på gardinerna, fäst vinylblommor i ett hörn av sovrummet eller använd en samling av små föremål för att ge rummen personlighet.

Give cuisine inspired motifs, widely used in kitchen decor, a modern touch by etching them on the glass.

On donne un air moderne aux motifs s'inspirant de la gastronomie, très utilisés dans la décoration de la cuisine, en les gravant à l'acide sur une surface en verre.

Geben Sie Motiven, die von der Gastronomie inspiriert sind und in der Kücheneinrichtung oft verwendet werden, ein modernes Flair, indem Sie in eine Glasscheibe ätzen.

Geef een modern tintje aan motieven die geïnspireerd zijn op de gastronomie en die veelvuldig gebruikt worden in de inrichting van de keuken, door ze af te drukken glas door middel van zuurgraveren.

Imprime un aire moderno a los motivos inspirados en la gastronomía, muy usados en la decoración de la cocina, aplicándolos sobre un cristal mediante el proceso de grabado al ácido.

Dai un'aria moderna ai motivi ispirati alla gastronomia, molto usati nell'arredo della cucina, applicandoli su un vetro con la tecnica di incisione tramite acido.

Dê um ar moderno aos motivos inspirados na gastronomia, muito usados na decoração da cozinha, aplicando-os sobre um vidro recorrendo ao processo de gravação a ácido.

Skänk ett modernt utseende åt gastronomiska motiv, som ofta används för att dekorera kök, genom att trycka dem på glas genom gravering med syra.

Give the most traditional pieces a light-hearted edge.

Comment apporter un brin d'insouciance dans les pièces plus traditionnelles.

Injizieren Sie ein bisschen Heiterkeit in die traditionellsten Objekte.

Geef de meest traditionele elementen iets informeels.

Inyecta un poco de desenfado en las piezas más tradicionales.

Trasmetti un tocco di leggerezza ai pezzi più tradizionali.

Torne as peças tradicionais mais ousadas.

Ge de mest traditionella föremålen en informell känsla.

Combine eye-catching tablecloths, with plates with the same design pattern, or are completely white that make the table stand out.

Les nappes avec des imprimés très voyants peuvent être accompagnées d'assiettes design ornées des mêmes motifs ou complètement blanches pour qu'elles ressortent sur la table.

Kombinieren Sie sehr auffallend gemusterte Tischdecken mit Geschirr, das dasselbe Muster trägt, oder mit einem vollkommen weißen Service, das sich vom Tisch optisch abhebt.

Combineer tafelkleden met een heel opvallende opdruk met design borden met hetzelfde motief of helemaal wit, zodat ze op tafel opvallen.

Combina los manteles con un estampado muy llamativo, con platos de diseño que lleven el mismo motivo o sean completamente blancos para que resalten en la mesa.

Combina le tovaglie con una stampa di impatto, con piatti di design che riprendano lo stesso motivo o totalmente bianchi per dare risalto al tavolo.

Combine as toalhas de mesa com estampados chamativos, com pratos design que tenham o mesmo motivo ou com pratos completamente brancos para que sobressaiam na mesa.

Kombinera dukar med speciella mönster med designtallrikar med samma motiv eller helt vita tallrikar som sticker ut på bordet.

Leave glassware with original shapes and colors in view so that they become decorative elements.

Les verres design, aux formes originales et aux couleurs vives, deviennent des objets de décoration.

Stellen Sie Designergläser mit originellen Formen und auffallenden Farben als dekorative Objekte sichtbar auf.

Laat design glaswerk in het zicht staan, met originele vormen en opvallende kleuren, zodat ze de functie hebben van decoratieve voorwerpen.

Deja a la vista la cristalería de diseño, con formas originales y colores destacados para que funcionen como objetos decorativos.

Lascia in vista i bicchieri di design dalle forme originali e dai colori inconsueti, si trasformeranno in oggetti decorativi.

Deixe à vista objectos design em vidro, com formas originais e cores chamativas para que funcionem como elementos decorativos.

Låt designglas i originella former och färger stå framme som dekorativa föremål.

Minimalist ornaments are ideal for the kitchen because they maintain the clean aesthetic required in this space.

Les éléments décoratifs minimalistes sont parfaits pour la cuisine, car ils respectent l'esthétique soignée requise par cet espace.

Für die Küche sind minimalistische Ziergegenstände geeignet, weil sie die Ästhetik der Sauberkeit, die dieser Raum verlangt, beibehalten.

Minimalistische details zijn ideaal voor de keuken omdat ze de esthetiek en netheid die in deze ruimte vereist zijn intact laten.

Los adornos minimalistas son idóneos para la cocina porque mantienen la estética de pulcritud que requiere este espacio.

Gli oggetti di ispirazione minimalista sono adatti alla cucina perché mantengono l'estetica di purezza che richiede questo spazio.

Os elementos minimalistas são ideais para a cozinha porque mantêm a estética de simplicidade que se pretende neste espaço.

Minimalistiska prydnadsföremål är idealiska i köket eftersom de upprätthåller den rena estetik som detta rum kräver.

In industrial-style kitchens or kitchens with one predominant color, apply touches of color using gadgets and exposed dishes.

Dans les cuisines en style industriel ou dominées par une seule couleur, les gadgets et la vaisselle, laissés à l'extérieur, apportent des touches de couleur.

In Küchen von industriellem Zuschnitt oder in denen, in denen ein einziger Farbton vorherrscht, bringen Sie eine farbige Note durch *gadgets* und Schüsseln, die Sie sichtbar aufstellen.

Breng in de keukens met een industrieel ontwerp of waar een enkele toon overheerst kleurrijke accenten aan door *gadgets* en schalen in het zicht te zetten.

En las cocinas de corte industrial o en las que predomina un solo tono, aplica notas de color a través de los *gadgets* y fuentes que puedas dejar al descubierto.

Nelle cucine di taglio industriale o in cui predomina un solo tono, applica delle note di colore tramite i *gadget* e piatti che possono essere lasciati in vista.

Nas cozinhas com estilo industrial ou naquelas em predomina um só tom, aplique notas de cor através de *gadgets* e peças que possam ficar à vista.

I industriella kök eller kök där en färg dominerar kan man lägga till färginslag genom olika apparater och skålar som kan stå framme.

To give a few rooms of the house a Provencal air, display white porcelain dishes and wicker baskets, which are very practical.

La vaisselle en porcelaine blanche et les paniers en osier, très pratiques, donnent un air provençal à certains endroits de la maison.

Um einigen Räumen im Haus einen Hauch der Provence zu verleihen, stellen Sie weiße Schüsseln und Strohkörbchen auf, sie sind außerdem sehr praktisch.

Zet praktische, witte porseleinen schalen en rieten manden neer voor een Provençaals accent in bepaalde vertrekken van de woning.

Para dar un aire provenzal a algunos ambientes de la casa, deja fuentes de porcelana blanca y canastas de mimbre a la vista, muy prácticas.

Per dare un'aria provenzale ad alcuni ambienti della casa, lascia ciotole di porcellana bianca e ceste di vimini a vista, sono molto pratiche.

Para dar um ar rústico a alguns espaços da casa, deixe peças de porcelana branca e cestas de vime à vista, muito práticas.

För att ge ett provencalskt intryck till några av husets rum kan man ställa fram porslinsskålar och rottingkorgar, som är mycket praktiska.

Place pots in wooden crates, crocheted covers or instead use a brass watering can.

Vous pouvez utiliser comme cache-pot des caisses en bois, des housses faites au crochet ou bien un arrosoir en laiton.

Stellen Sie Blumentöpfe in Holzkästen oder gehäkelte Hüllen oder ersetzen Sie sie durch eine Messinggießkanne.

Plaats bloempotten in houten kisten, gehaakte hoezen of vervang ze door een messing gieter.

Coloca las macetas dentro de cajones de madera, fundas de ganchillo o sustitúyelas por una regadera de latón.

Sistema i vasi dentro scatole di legno, contenitori realizzati all'uncinetto oppure sostituiscili con un annaffiatoio in latta.

Coloque os vasos dentro de caixas de madeira, decore-os com fronhas de croché ou opte por regadores em latão.

Placera blomkrukor i trälådor eller virkade fordral eller byt ut dem mot en vattenkanna av stål.

Make doors stand out with unusual handles, whether old-style wrought iron or a piece of hanging glass.

Les portes peuvent être valorisées par des poignées particulières, à l'ancienne en fer forgé ou ornées d'un pendentif en verre.

Heben Sie die Türen durch besonders gestaltete Klinken, entweder aus Schmiedeeisen nach altem Stil oder mit einem hängenden Glastropfen, hervor.

Laat deuren opvallen door middel van een deurknop met een bijzonder ontwerp, bijvoorbeeld van smeedwerk in oude stijl of met een glazen onderdeel eraan.

Resalta las puertas con manillas con un diseño especial, ya sean de forja al estilo antiguo o con una pieza de cristal colgante.

Dai risalto alle porte con maniglie dalla forma speciale, in ferro battuto che richiama il passato o appendendovi un pezzo di cristallo o vetro.

Faça sobressair as portas utilizando maçanetas com design especial, sejam de metal forjado ao estilo antigo ou com elementos em vidro.

Framhäv dörrarna med handtag i speciell design, antingen av järn i gammal stil eller med ett stycke glas som hänger.

Decorate the bathroom with necklaces, bracelets and earrings hanging from a small floor stand or from the edge of the mirror.

Vous pouvez décorer la salle de bain avec des colliers, des bracelets et des pendentifs accrochés à un support sur pied ou au cadre du miroir.

Dekorieren Sie das Bad mit Halsketten, Armbändern und Ohrringen, die an einem kleinen Ständer oder am Spiegelrahmen hängen.

Richt de badkamer in door kettingen, armbanden en oorbellen aan een kleine staander of aan de rand van de spiegel te hangen.

Decora el baño con collares, pulseras y pendientes colgados de un pequeño soporte de pie o del borde del espejo.

Decora il bagno con collane, bracciali e orecchini appesi a un piccolo supporto dotato di base o al bordo dello specchio.

Decore a casa de banho com colares, pulseiras e pendentes suspensos num pequeno suporte de pé ou na moldura do espelho.

Dekorera badrummet med halsband, armband och örhängen i en liten ställning eller vid sidan av spegeln.

Shells are ideal for decorating the bathroom, not only for their obvious resistance to moisture but also for creating a marine environment.

Les coquillages s'adaptent bien à la décoration de la salle de bain : ils résistent à l'humidité et ils évoquent le milieu marin.

Schneckenhäuser und Muscheln sind ideal, um das Bad zu dekorieren, nicht nur wegen ihrer offensichtlichen Resistenz gegen Feuchtigkeit, sondern auch weil sie Assoziationen an das Meer hervorrufen.

Slakkenhuizen en schelpen zijn ideaal om de badkamer mee te versieren, niet alleen vanwege hun evidente vochtbestendigheid, maar ook vanwege de associatie met de zee die zij oproepen.

Las caracolas y conchas de mar son ideales para decorar el baño, no solo por su obvia resistencia a la humedad, sino también por su evocación del ambiente marino.

Le conchiglie sono ideali per decorare il bagno, non solo per l'ovvia resistenza all'umidità, ma anche per l'evocazione dell'ambiente marino.

Os búzios e conchas do mar são ideais para decorar a casa de banho, não só pela sua óbvia resistência à humidade mas também pela sua evocação ao ambiente marinho.

Snäckor är perfekta för att dekorera badrummet, inte bara för att de står emot fukten utan för att de påminner om havet.

As in spas or hotels, rolls hand towels and leave them in view the creating different combinations of colors.

Wie in den *spas* oder Hotels rollen Sie die Handtücher zusammen und legen Sie sie nach Farben geordnet sichtbar aus.

Comme dans les spas ou dans les hôtels, vous pouvez rouler les serviettes et les laisser à l'extérieur, formant ainsi des compositions de couleurs.

Rol gastenhanddoekjes op, net als in *spa's* of hotels, en leg ze in het zicht, zo dat ze kleurencomposities vormen.

Como en los *spas* o los hoteles, haz rollitos con las toallas de mano y déjalas a la vista formando composiciones de colores.

Come in una *spa* o in hotel, arrotola gli asciugamani e lasciali in vista formando composizioni di colori.

Como nos *spas* ou nos hotéis, enrole as toalhas de mão e deixe-as à vista formando composições de cores.

Du kan göra rullar av handdukarna, som på ett spa eller hotell, och lämna dem framme arrangerade i olika färgkompositioner.

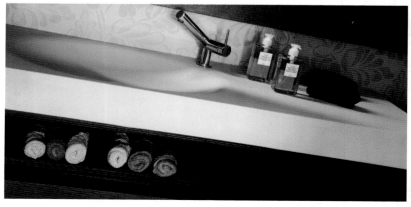